ASSESSING WOMAN
BATTERING IN
MENTAL HEALTH
SERVICES

■■ BOOKS UNDER THE GENERAL EDITORSHIP OF JON R. CONTE

Hate Crimes: Confronting Violence Against Lesbians and Gay Men
edited by Gregory M. Herek and Kevin T. Berrill

Legal Responses to Wife Assault: Current Trends and Evaluation
edited by N. Zoe Hilton

The Male Survivor: The Impact of Sexual Abuse
by Matthew Parynik Mendel

The Child Sexual Abuse Custody Dispute
Annotated Bibliography
by Wendy Deaton, Suzanne Long, Holly A. Magana,
and Julie Robbins

The Survivor's Guide
by Sharice Lee

Psychotherapy and Mandated Reporting of Child Maltreatment
by Murray Levine and Howard J. Doueck

Sexual Abuse in Nine North American Cultures:
Treatment and Prevention
edited by Lisa Aronson Fontes

The Role of Social Support in Preventing Child Maltreatment
by Ross A. Thompson

Intimate Betrayal: Understanding and Responding to the
Trauma of Acquaintance Rape
by Vernon R. Wiehe and Ann L. Richards

Violence Against Women Research: Methodological and Personal Perspectives
edited by Martin D. Schwartz

Sibling Abuse: Hidden Physical, Emotional, and Sexual Trauma
by Vernon R. Wiehe

Children Acting Sexually Aggressively: Coming to Understand Them
by Sharon K. Araji

Assessing Woman Battering in Mental Health Services
by Edward W. Gondolf

ASSESSING WOMAN
BATTERING IN
MENTAL HEALTH
SERVICES

Edward W. Gondolf

SAGE Publications
International Educational and Professional Publisher
Thousand Oaks London New Delhi

For information:

SAGE Publications, Inc.
2455 Teller Road
Thousand Oaks, California 91320
E-mail: order@sagepub.com

SAGE Publications Ltd.
6 Bonhill Street
London EC2A 4PU
United Kingdom

SAGE Publications India Pvt. Ltd.
M-32 Market
Greater Kailash I
New Delhi 110 048 India

Printed in the United States of America

Library of Congress Cataloging-in-Publication Data

Gondolf, Edward W., 1948-
    Assessing woman battering in mental health services / by Edward W. Gondolf.
        p.   cm.
    Includes bibliographical references and index.
    ISBN 0-7619-1107-3 (cloth: acid-free paper). —
    ISBN 0-7619-1108-1 (pbk.: acid-free paper)
    1. Abused women—Mental health services.   I. Title.
    RC569.5.F3G657 1997
    362.2'7—dc21   97-4882

This book is printed on acid-free paper.

98 99 00 01 02 03 10 9 8 7 6 5 4 3 2 1

Acquiring Editor:	C. Terry Hendrix
Editorial Assistant:	Dale Mary Grenfell
Production Editor:	Sherrise M. Purdum
Production Assistant:	Karen Wiley
Typesetter/Designer:	Danielle Dillahunt
Indexer:	Edwin Durbin
Cover Designer:	Candice Harman
Print Buyer:	Anna Chin

Contents

■ Acknowledgments   vii

■ Introduction   ix

I. UNDERLYING ISSUES FACING ASSESSMENT

■ 1. Addressing Differences and Barriers   3
    Differences in Perspective   5
    Organizational Barriers   14
    Conclusion   21

■ 2. Moving Toward Collaboration   23
    Existing Cooperation   24
    Examples of Collaboration   28
    Toward Collaboration   30
    Conclusion   38

II. TOOLS FOR IMPROVED ASSESSMENT

■ 3. Case Studies of Mental Health Evaluations   43
    Commitment of a Battered Woman   45
    Evaluation of a Recently Battered Woman   48
    Evaluation of a Woman With Multiple Problems 55
    Conclusion   62

■■ 4. Procedures for Assessing Woman Battering   65
     Screening Questions   68
     Assessment Instruments   69
     Abuse History   72
     Safety Planning   77
     Diagnosis   79
     Reporting and Documentation   90
     Conclusion   92

■■ 5. Recognizing the Strengths of Battered Women   95
     With Angela Browne, PhD
     Recognizing Strengths   97
     Toward a Survivor Theory   103
     Strengths Inventory   105
     Conclusion   109

III. OTHER CONSIDERATIONS IN ASSESSMENT

■■ 6. Appreciating Diversity Among Battered Women   113
     African American Women   119
     Latina Women   122
     Native American Women   124
     Asian Women   126
     Immigrant Women   128
     Conclusion   131

■■ 7. Identifying and Assessing Men Who Batter   132
     Identifying Battering   134
     Assessing Psychopathology   141
     Clinical Response   145
     Conclusion   154

■■ Appendix: A Survey of
Battered Women's Advocates   157
     With Susan Schechter, MSW

■■ Recommended Bibliography   163

■■ References   169

■■ Index   181

■■ About the Authors   187

Acknowledgments

This book represents the collective effort of a variety of individuals and agencies. The National Resource Center on Domestic Violence (NRC) sponsored the development of the book through a grant from the U.S. Department of Health and Human Services. Anne Menard, the director of NRC, helped coordinate and guide the project. Susan Schechter, of the University of Iowa and a consultant to NRC, assisted in formulating the issues and offering extensive comments and editing. In collaboration with NRC, Susan also devised and conducted a survey of battered women's advocates that focused on and illustrated the issues.

Carole Warshaw, a practicing psychiatrist in Chicago, offered advice and knowledge on the perspective and practice of mental health clinicians. The work of Angela Browne, a psychologist known for her study of battered women, forms the basis of the discussion of battered women's strengths. Beth Richie, a professor at Hunter College with expertise in gender and race, provided comments and suggestions for Chapter 6, "Appreciating Diversity Among Battered Women." Many other advocates and mental health practitioners indirectly contributed their experience and efforts through conferences, writings, and personal conversations.

Staff and graduate students at the Mid-Atlantic Addiction Training Institute helped collect research articles, proofread drafts, and make corrections in the text: Crystal Deemer, Jewel Lee Douherty, Alicia Dohn, and Patty Pierson.

I am immensely grateful to all these individuals for their assistance and support. I feel fortunate to have had the opportunity to work with and learn from such a collection of thoughtful, dedicated, and insightful people. I thank especially the NRC for its foresight in conceiving of this important project and for helping to make it a reality.

Introduction

■ PURPOSE

The need for collaboration between mental health clinicians and battered women's advocates is increasingly apparent. The number of battered women who appear in mental health settings is very high, a result of the psychological effect of battering on women. The response to these women's mental health problems is not always appropriate or safe, however. Mental health clinicians may not identify and address the battering, or they may misdiagnose and mistreat a woman because they do not fully grasp the nature of the abuse.

Part of the difficulty lies in applying the conventional perspective and practices of clinical psychology to what battered women's advocates have long argued is a deep-seated social problem. Men who batter often escalate their abuse in response to a woman's seeking help. A battered woman who seeks help may be subjected to additional condemnation, threats, retaliation, stalking, custody problems, and financial loss that may further her psychological distress, as well as endanger her physically.

In recent years, advocates and clinicians alike have been working to develop a response to battered women that considers both their psychological needs and their immediate social circumstances.[1] The National Resource Center on Domestic Violence (NRC) commissioned this book as part of this ongoing effort. The objective of the book is to enhance the response of mental health clinicians to woman battering.[2] The primary aim is to increase the identification and assessment of battered women in mental health services, and as a result increase the prospects for referral to battered women's programs or mental health treatment specific to battered women's needs. The broader purpose is to raise awareness of the clinical issues associated with woman battering and to advance collaboration that should help address those issues.

This book represents a compilation of much of the expertise and innovation devised by the woman-battering field to work with battered women safely and judiciously. More specifically, it examines the following:

- The differences in perspective and the structural obstacles that have limited the exchange between mental health clinicians and battered women's advocates
- Specific tools, instruments, procedures, and cautions designed to increase the identification and improve the assessment of woman battering in mental health services
- Additional considerations and complications involved in assessing woman battering, such as racial differences and substance abuse

This book is an important but preliminary step in improving the response of mental health services to woman battering. Ultimately, cross-training, professional directives, collaborative treatments, policy changes, and specialized research that draws on the experience and expertise of battered women's advocates need to be expanded.

■■ PERSPECTIVE

Advocates' Expertise

The perspective of this book is primarily from the vantage point of battered women's advocates. The book attempts to bring the lessons, experience, and knowledge from the woman battering field to those working in mental health services. Nearly 20 years of work with battered women has led to established practices and considerations that are increasingly useful to other fields. Safety planning, for instance, has grown out of an understanding of battered women's lives and the practical experience of attempting to help them. The growing body of research on woman battering is referred to in the book to help substantiate and elaborate this practical expertise.

The mental health field has also contributed to this growing body of knowledge. Several clinical psychologists and psychiatrists have worked extensively with battered women and served these women as advocates as well as therapists. In the process, they have substantially contributed to the understanding of the effect of battering and abuse on women and to the development of mental health interventions for these women. These practitioners have also assisted professional associations in the mental health field to establish protocols and policies dealing with woman battering.

Battered women's advocates, in collaboration with domestic violence researchers and clinicians, have developed a number of practical innovations useful to the mental health field. The most prominent of these are

- Screening techniques and procedures
- Identification of various types of abuse
- Safety planning for battered women
- Alternative diagnoses and descriptors
- Recognition of the strengths of battered women
- "Empowering" interactions and counseling
- Collaborative interventions and treatment of women

This book offers procedures and examples of these important contributions.

Advocates and Clinicians

The book attempts to build a bridge between battered women's advocates and mental health clinicians. *Battered women's advocates* refers here to individuals who work to provide services, resources, and counseling to the women victims of battering and to improve the community's response to all abused women. Advocates not only are involved in direct service delivery such as maintaining residential shelters, they

also are active in prompting more effective and comprehensive responses from other agencies, such as the police, the courts, and hospitals.
They may work as shelter staff, group counselors, court liaisons, or
professional trainers.

Mental health clinicians refers to those who provide mental health
services in the form of intake and assessment, diagnoses and treatment,
and referral and casework for those with emotional, psychiatric, or
relational problems. They primarily include psychiatrists, clinical psychologists, nurse clinicians, trained counselors, and social workers.
The settings for their work vary widely: mental health clinics, psychiatric hospitals, family service centers, group homes, and private offices
or centers. Treatment also may include drug therapy, individual counseling, couples or family counseling, and group counseling in an inpatient or outpatient facility. Variations exist across payment systems as
well: privately funded versus publicly funded facilities, health management organizations versus treatment options supported by public
assistance.

This book attempts to focus on advocates' and mental health clinicians' needs to illustrate the major issues in dealing with woman battering. The range of mental health settings raises a diversity of needs and
interventions. What is done in a psychiatric emergency room to assess
woman battering may be very different from what is done in a family
counseling session. What is presented in the book will, therefore, need to be
adapted to the various settings and functions of mental health clinicians
and to their experience with and knowledge of woman battering.

▉ CONTENTS

Overview

The book is organized into three parts: one addressing issues that underlie inappropriate assessment, a second dealing with assessment procedures, and a third examining broader considerations needed in assessing
different situations and circumstances. The overall thesis is that a woman
battering protocol, attending to the social circumstances of battered
women, should be implemented within a process of organizational
development that builds toward collaboration and change.

Part I, "Underlying Issues Facing Assessment," discusses problems that contribute to inappropriate or inadequate assessment of battered women. This part includes two chapters:

- Chapter 1, "Addressing Differences and Barriers," examines the major differences between the medical perspective that influences mental health clinicians and the victim-perpetrator image held by the majority of battered women's advocates. It also considers the aspects of the evaluation process and the organization of mental health services that often retraumatize battered women or overlook their abusive situations. This chapter concludes with the possibility of a new model emerging from the mutual interest in the effect of trauma on women and by posing a battered women protocol that helps ensure the identification and assessment of battered women.
- Chapter 2, "Moving Toward Collaboration," discusses some of the existing cooperative efforts between battered women's programs and mental health services. It also recommends strategies for developing more extensive collaboration that helps implement and maintain a battered women protocol. Collaboration would also help to develop new joint treatment ventures that serve battered women in the community more effectively.

Part II presents specific tools, instruments, guides, and procedures to improve the identification and assessment of battered women in mental health services.

- Chapter 3, "Case Studies of Mental Health Evaluations," analyzes three mental health evaluations of battered women from the perspective of both mental health clinicians and battered women's advocates. These case studies point out opportunities for negotiating or resolving differences and obstacles.
- Chapter 4, "Procedures for Assessing Woman Battering," introduces screening questions, assessment scales, a history inventory, safety planning procedures, diagnostic options, and record-keeping guidelines that might be incorporated into the mental health evaluation process.
- Chapter 5, "Recognizing the Strengths of Battered Women," provides a rationale for shifting the focus from psychopathology to survivor

strengths, and it provides questions and procedures for conducting an assessment of strengths.

Part III raises additional considerations involved in improving the assessment of woman battering.

- Chapter 6, "Appreciating Racial Diversity Among Battered Women," points out special considerations in assessing women from different racial backgrounds and other influential social or personal situations. African American and Hispanic women, for instance, may warrant different clinical responses and different strategies in safety planning because of their unique social circumstances.
- Chapter 7, "Identifying and Assessing Men Who Batter," reviews purported characteristics of batterers, batterers' minimization and justifications of abuse, and the need to hold such men accountable for their actions. It also reviews the issues associated with contacting the battered women involved and assisting with their safety.

A recommended bibliography of additional research and clinical articles concludes the book. The articles might be useful for mental health clinicians for their own reading after a training conference, or to help answer inquiries and requests for further information about responding to woman battering in mental health services.

A Note About Treatment

The actual treatment of battered women in mental health services is beyond the scope of this book, which focuses primarily on the initial assessment. Treatment, however, raises many issues that need to be addressed.

- How do women differ in their response to abuse and their need for treatment?
- How is a woman's safety to be addressed while in treatment?
- What is the role of battered women's programs in mental health treatment?
- What kind and how much medication is appropriate for a battered woman?

- What kind of referral to and consultation with battered women's programs are necessary?
- What is the role of battered women's support groups, advocacy, and shelter residences in treatment?

Some of these issues are at least partially addressed in the articles recommended in the bibliography. Also, several books are now available that specifically deal with treatment for battered women—treatment that acknowledges their abuse and moves them toward healing and social support. In particular, *Empowering and Healing the Battered Woman* by Mary Ann Dutton (1992b) offers an excellent guide for conducting therapy with battered women.

Another related use of assessment for battered women is in evaluations for legal situations: divorce hearings, custody cases, and self-defense charges. Expert testimony and forensic work may require some of the same considerations involved in assessing a woman to determine appropriate treatment and service. Conducting an extensive abuse history, dangerousness assessment, safety plan, and appropriate diagnosis, for instance, would be warranted. The court often has different standards for evaluation, however. The findings of an evaluation must address certain provisions in the law, such as *mens rae,* requiring a person to be capable of understanding responsibility for a crime. The presentation of an evaluation in court also requires a special form, expertise, and finding not addressed in the scope of this book. Those wanting more information on mental health assessment and legal issues might contact the National Clearinghouse for the Defense of Battered Women, based in Philadelphia (phone 215-351-0010), for more advice in this regard.

◼◼ USING THIS BOOK

Training Uses

The use of this book may depend on the relationship of battered women's programs to mental health services in their respective communities. On the one hand, some battered women's advocates have already built collaborative relationships with mental health clinicians to serve the needs of battered women in shelters and the community. Battered women's programs may have staff psychologists or consulting psychologists who review the mental health needs of shelter residents and provide treatment consistent with the shelter's programs and aims. Some advocates also maintain linkages with mental health services, permitting the shelter to refer battered women to those services.

On the other hand, some battered women's advocates continue to question the collaboration with mental health services because of the consequences that mental health diagnoses sometimes hold for battered women. They also resist the encroachment of mental health treatment into their ongoing work with battered women, because some psychological assessments appear to blame abused women or lessen batterers' responsibility for the violence. Some battered women report being retraumatized in mental health clinics or psychological facilities and resist further involvement with them.

Most advocates find themselves somewhere between full collaboration and outright caution. They make referrals to supportive mental health clinicians and are involved in training mental health clinicians in their communities, much as other advocates train police or nurses.

These materials may be used in several different ways to meet the range of program and community situations suggested above. They may be used

- As the basis of a workshop for mental health clinicians or as supplemental material in a workshop
- As a resource given directly to mental health clinicians who inquire about woman battering or who have some contact with battered women's programs
- As a source to address specific needs, objectives, or requests; the assessment tools and safety planning portion, for instance, might be distributed to mental health clinicians currently receiving shelter referrals
- As a reference for clinicians already familiar with woman battering who want more information on ways to respond to the problem
- As a reference for local mental health, family service, and psychological associations that may have representatives on a communitywide domestic violence task, policy, or study group
- As an overview to familiarize battered women's staff with mental health issues they may want to address
- As a text in clinical psychology, social work, or counseling programs; the book offers an efficient compilation of available information and a synthesis of issues facing the field

The information presented here is probably best introduced in the context of cross-training experiences and a sustained exchange between battered women's advocates and mental health clinicians in the community. In this way, a more substantial understanding of the issues and dialogue to advance such understanding is likely to evolve.

■■ NOTES

1. A task group of the American Psychological Association recently completed a report of recommendations for clinicians dealing with family violence. The report offers an overview of several forms of family violence, including woman battering, with summaries of issues, general knowledge, and preferred practices. The report, *Violence and the Family: Report of the American Psychological Association Presidential Task Force on Violence and the Family* (American Psychological Association, 1996), is available from the American Psychological Association (order department: 1-800-374-2721). The recommended practices, although sensitive to the expertise of advocates, draw primarily from the perspective of clinical psychologists working against family violence and do not provide the details for a woman battering protocol or developing collaborations presented in this book.

2. The term *woman battering* is used through this book to refer to the physical abuse of women by their intimate male partners. The term *battering* may refer to a wide range of physical abuse, including grabbing, pushing, shoving, slapping, punching, choking, pulling hair, burning, kicking, forced sex, using weapons, and throwing things. Physical battering is often accompanied by an array of controlling behavior and psychological abuse in the form of insults, accusations, threats, intimidation, financial control, and social isolation. Any level or combination of abuse can cause fear or control. Battered women sometimes refer to their partner as only having to clench his fist to invoke fear and get what he wants.

Woman battering is used instead of *domestic violence* because domestic violence may imply child abuse, elder abuse, or sibling abuse. Similarly, the terms *family violence* and *spouse abuse* imply assault among family members other than male violence against intimate female partners. Woman battering is distinguished from abuse among same-sex partners, other relatives, acquaintances, or strangers because it tends to have unique dynamics, effects, and problems. Many of the tools, however, such as safety planning, can be applied to any adult relationships characterized by abuse.

PART I

Underlying Issues
Facing Assessment

1

Addressing Differences and Barriers

Seeing Two Trees

A poet looks at a tree and beholds an enthralling wonder of nature, whereas a carpenter may see so many feet of lumber. How do two people look at the same thing and see two entirely different things? How we respond is influenced, at least in part, by our vantage point, our training, and the purpose of our work.

The response to battered women is similarly influenced by the professional setting that shapes it. The formal training and informal socialization in a particular setting help form the perspective or outlook one brings to a problem. What we "see"—or get to see—may be constrained by the organizational procedures, structures, and constraints of a setting. They tend to focus our view on one aspect of what we encounter.

It is helpful, therefore, to be aware of the influences our respective professional settings may impose. In that way, we may get a better idea about why we see wondrous nature instead of board feet, or vice versa. We may also be able to see the broader possibilities of what is before us.

Two Steps Toward Change

One of the first steps in developing more appropriate responses to battered women is to identify the differences in perspective between battered women's advocates and mental health clinicians. Considering differences in perspective appears to facilitate discussion, training, and referrals across fields. It can help mental health clinicians grasp the concerns of battered women's advocates. Exposing the differences can also further identify intersections in the two fields that might form the basis of more collaborative programming and help formulate a broader framework of understanding.

A second related step in enhancing the response of mental health services to battered women is to address the organizational barriers that battered women encounter in mental health services. These barriers include an evaluation process that may inadvertently neglect a woman's abuse, label her as *mentally ill,* or aggravate her emotional pain and fear. Moreover, many battered women may not have access to mental health services or the finances to pay for them. Others encounter a professional culture that may be intimidating or upsetting. Some organizational changes are therefore needed along with training and referrals. Ultimately, mental health services and battered women's programs might build collaborative relationships that sustain innovation and change.

The first section of this chapter reviews fundamental assumptions shaping the perspectives of the woman battering and mental health fields. It contrasts what is commonly referred to as the *medical model* (which forms the basis of most mental health diagnoses, billings, and treatments) with the perspective underlying much of the battered women's movement.[1] The prospects for new models that may accommodate the essentials of several perspectives while honoring the practical needs of battered women are also discussed. The second section, focusing on organizational barriers, examines the inappropriate treatment that battered women often encounter and the evaluation process that partially accounts for it. The section also introduces the notion of a battered women protocol as a beginning means to counter these barriers and open the door to further collaboration with battered women's programs.

■■ DIFFERENCES IN PERSPECTIVE

A Survey of Battered Women's Programs

To understand the relationship of battered women's programs and mental health services better, the National Resource Center on Domestic Violence initiated a survey of state domestic violence coalitions in the spring of 1994. These coalitions coordinate the battered women's programs in their states and represent them to their respective state legislatures. The survey was conducted through a mailed questionnaire to the 50 state coalitions, with 60% of the coalitions responding. A portion of the survey comprised open-ended questions inquiring about major problems between battered women's programs and mental health services. The responses were categorized and tabulated by research consultants. (Details of the methodology and conclusions of the study appear in the appendix.)

The survey respondents believe that the different perceptions, training, and priorities of mental health clinicians limit their understanding of woman battering and, to a certain extent, make them resistant to the expertise that advocates have developed and attempt to share (see Table 1.1). The respondents were particularly concerned that mental health clinicians do not fully understand woman battering and that they do not seek the knowledge of advocates on this subject. Over half (53%) of the state coalitions felt that mental health professionals do not understand woman battering issues and dynamics. Their comments were emphatic:

"They (mental health clinicians) don't seem to appreciate that being battered often leads to various underlying mental health problems. End the battering and often the other issues disappear."

"They lack awareness of the power, control, and basic dynamics of violence against women and children. They embrace a medical model that often gets in the way of dealing with the violence in women's lives."

"They have little appreciation for the need to promote social change in order to deal with domestic violence."

Unfortunately, these differences contribute to what some coalitions considered the fundamental barrier between the two fields—a lack of

TABLE 1.1 Differences and Barriers With Mental Health Professionals

Response	# of States Responding	Percentage of States
Mental health clinicians do not understand woman battering issues or dynamics	16	53%
Mental health clinicians do not accept battered women's advocates as professionals	11	36%
Inappropriate mental health treatment for woman battering (dangerous, misdiagnosis, etc.)	24	80%
Lack of access to mental health services (no transportation, high cost, waiting lists, etc.)	15	50%

NOTE: 30 States responded; $n = 30$

trust. As one advocate noted in the survey, "It can be summed up this way: There is a lack of TRUST between the women and professionals." About a third (36%) of the coalitions felt that mental health professionals do not respect battered women's advocates. Respondents to the survey claim that "there is no recognition for the work of battered women's advocates." Advocates felt that mental health clinicians consider advocates to be of a lower status. According to one state coalition, "mental health professionals seem hung-up on the letters after a person's name, rather than respond to the expertise they achieve through working." As one coalition staff observes, "mental health professionals do not trust battered women nor battered women's advocates' skills."

Differing Experience and Training

The apparent differences in perspective between the woman battering and mental health fields appear to stem from contrasting historical development, theoretical frameworks, and essential objectives. Battered women's programs, on the one hand, have developed a largely experiential knowledge base over the last 20 years (Dobash & Dobash, 1992; Schechter, 1982). They have forged a unique perspective on the dynamics, effect, and nature of woman battering that has had a profound effect

	Battered Women Programs	Mental Health Services
Analysis	Sociological analysis	Medical model
Problem	Social problem	Psychopathology/ personality disorder
Dynamics	Male power and control	Interactive family system
Objective	Safety and empowerment	Mental stability and coherence
Service	Safety, resources, sanctions	Medication, psychotherapy, hospitalization
Social Aim	Institutional reform and social change	Individual coping with stressors and adjustment to society

Figure 1.1. Differing Perspectives Between Battered Women Programs and Mental Health Services

on how other community agencies, particularly the criminal justice system, respond to incidents of woman abuse. Volunteers and paraprofessionals have played a large part in developing and sustaining battered women's programs and have emerged as a grassroots movement (Dobash & Dobash, 1992). The majority of battered women's programs approach battering primarily as a social problem in which empowerment counseling and establishing personal safety are essential.

Mental health clinicians, on the other hand, are professionally obligated to develop a psychiatric diagnosis and prescribe appropriate therapy toward alleviating the diagnosed pathology (Gondolf, 1990) or related dysfunction. A diversity of theoretical frameworks guides treatment ranging from psychodynamic to family systems theory, but fundamental to the mental health approach is a medical model that generally treats an individual's psychological and organic processes. Mental health services, and medical services in general, devise their treatments largely on the basis of scientific experimentation and rely on a system of credentialed expertise and authority to disperse those treatments.

As a result of their different roots, advocates and clinicians may approach battered women differently (see Figure 1.1). Battered women's advocates tend to rely on a sociological analysis, see power and control behind much of the abuse, believe criminal and social sanctions are needed to interrupt the violence and establish safety, and assert the need of battered women for support that enables them to make constructive decisions and obtain resources to carry those out. Early identification and decisive intervention are essential to avoid escalation of the violence.

Mental health clinicians, by contrast, tend to define the problem more narrowly. A woman's pathology may provoke or lead her into violent situations or contribute to dysfunctional family interactions that give rise to abuse. The interactive family system, of which the woman is a part, may itself need treatment or intervention. Moreover, a battered woman may suffer from dissociative, paranoid, or emotional disorders, or from dependent or borderline personality disorder, as a result of long-term abuse. These disorders may make her more "victim prone"— and therefore, highly susceptible to abusive men. The battered woman needs to be diagnosed and treated for such disorders through appropriate medication, psychotherapy, and/or inpatient care.

The Medical Model

The mental health field is admittedly diverse and changing. A variety of multifaceted treatments is being developed for the growing number of specialized disorders and problems. Nevertheless, a few outstanding assumptions appear to characterize the mental health approach to woman battering, and clients in general. Social theorists argue that contemporary mental health services are dominated by a medical model that views mental problems as having a physiological basis (Conrad & Schneider, 1985; Gondolf, 1990; Warshaw, 1989, 1993). The predominance of this model is in part related to three trends: the backlash against the minimally successful efforts of the community mental health movement, the advances in psychopharmacology that have brought more potent and less deleterious medication, and the biological research that points to a genetic component in mental illness.

The *medical model* assumes that the patient's symptoms and behavioral problems can be traced to an organic or biological dysfunction within the individual. Various social circumstances may act as stressors to precipitate or exacerbate the disorder, but the underlying cause is the illness itself. Moreover, an individual is more likely to act violently when suffering from a major disorder. Those persons with more than one disorder, such as depression and alcoholism, are likely to be the most violent or the most vulnerable to violence (Bland & Orn, 1986). In many cases, it might therefore be assumed that the violence will subside if the mental disorder can be treated successfully.

Victims of violence with a mental disorder or problem may be at risk in part because of their disorder. They may be overly dependent on undesirable peers, or subject themselves to dangerous circumstances because of a personality disorder. A psychotic or depressive disorder might manifest itself in offensive behavior that provokes retaliation or abuse. Victims of violence may, from this perspective, contribute to their abuse and be at least somewhat responsible for it.

Mental patients are likely to distort or misrepresent reality. Violence victims, as well as perpetrators, may be delusional, manipulating, or paranoid. Recent developments about repressed memory syndrome have brought claims of previous victimization into question. Mental health clinicians therefore may be suspicious of a patient's claims of abuse and battering and rely on the observations of anyone who accompanies the client or on the behavioral implications of the patient's disorder.

Some mental health clinicians openly question whether it is their role to assess or address an individual's social problems (Appelbaum, 1988). They see their responsibility as establishing a psychiatric diagnosis and administering appropriate therapy for that diagnosis. They are neither equipped nor charged with doing the social work needed to address interpersonal violence, marital problems, or poverty. That should be left to other institutions and agencies in the community that specialize in these areas.

Relationship Problems

This is not to suggest that mental health clinicians view the world with blinders. They are generally schooled in a systems analysis that places the individual in a more complex social context (Shea, 1988). The physiological, psychological, dyadic, family, societal, and existential aspects are considered to interact with one another in a reinforcing way. The physiological aspect of biomedical concern nevertheless remains at the center. This approach generally translates into a narrow set of treatment options—medication, individual therapy, and/or family counseling.

Within this perspective, relationship problems are usually indicated in diagnoses known as *V codes* (relationship problems warranting clinical attention) and are addressed through family counseling sessions. Marital problems, fights with relatives, acting-out behavior of the children, and even employment difficulties are frequently relegated to family counseling. This preferred treatment reflects the systems analysis that sees the family dimension as the most influential next to the physiological aspect. The family is the vestibule in which societal, existential, and psychological dimensions converge.

There is another fundamental reason for the popularity of family counseling as an encompassing social intervention. A substantial portion of mental patients is from multiproblem families with no clear "villain." In these families, several family members are abusive to others and suffer from their own mental disorders. Furthermore, alcoholism and drug addiction, chronic unemployment and poverty, and social isolation or violent subcultures may be at work. Family counseling represents one way to deal with this range of influences in a patient's life.

The Woman Battering Perspective

The relatively young field of woman battering has emerged within the last 20 years. It is rooted in two broad movements that have "discovered" the extent and effect of domestic violence (Tierney, 1982). First, the victims rights movement has brought increased public attention and aid to victims of violence (Walker, 1989). The criminal justice system, and community services in general, are more inclined to view the safety of victims, the psychological effects of victimization, and the resource needs of victimized individuals. Second, the women's movement made violence against women a political issue. Sexual assault and wife battering in particular were shown to be an extension of the secondary status of women in American society. This movement created nearly 1,000 women's shelters and safe homes in a decade, with little help or support from medical or mental health professionals at the time (Schechter, 1982). It was also instrumental in bringing fundamental changes to the criminal justice system, prompting the development of batterer programs and making woman battering a public health issue.

Fundamental to the orientation of battered women's advocates is that woman battering is a social problem. The startling statistic that at least one in three American wives is physically abused during her marriage seems to bear this out (Straus & Gelles, 1986). This pervasive violence is not merely the product of deviant or sick individuals. It has, in a sense, become the norm—it has been tolerated and accepted behavior. Woman battering, from this viewpoint, needs to be viewed clinically as a primary problem that warrants decisive social sanctions to interrupt and contain it. Perpetrators need, additionally, to learn alternative attitudes and behaviors. Simply treating their alcoholism or mental problems is not sufficient; these problems may compound the abuse, but are not their cause (see Gondolf, 1995). Victims, on the other hand, need special assistance in dealing with the minimization of violence and the fear of reprisals. They need assistance to see that they did not provoke the unpredictable violence—violence for which the perpetrator must take responsibility.

The dynamics of woman battering, from this perspective, are often described as the exploitation of power by the perpetrator over a victim. Even incidents that appear to be a "two-way" street take on a different character when put in a broader context. They usually fit into a long-standing pattern of control and domination on the part of the perpetrator (Walker, 1984). Violence on the victim's part may be seen primarily as an attempt at self-defense or as retaliation in the face of what may approximate a state of terror (Saunders, 1988). Moreover, the effect of the violence is generally not a clear two-way street; the woman is the one more likely to be severely injured.

Victim-Perpetrator Intervention

According to most battered women's advocates, the family counseling so often recommended by mental health clinicians is inappropriate as an initial intervention. Rather than woman battering being enmeshed in a dysfunctional family system, a perpetrator and a victim can usually be identified. To put them together into counseling is to imply that the victim is an accomplice and puts her at risk of future abuse if she discloses the truth (Bograd, 1984, 1992; Hansen, 1993; Kaufman, 1992). In fact, woman battering is likely to escalate and become more lethal if it is not decisively interrupted. In its sometimes cyclical nature, woman battering appears to have abated only to erupt more seriously later (Walker, 1979).

Woman battering must be seen as the crime that it is. Battered women's advocates have lobbied in recent years to establish arrest policies and criminal penalties for offenders that have brought increased reporting and decreased recidivism. The current concern is that punishment alone cannot stop woman battering. The next phase for the movement against woman battering is to organize a system of community services to intervene in woman battering cases. Preliminary research suggests that this multifaceted social intervention increases effectiveness (see Bowker 1983; Edleson & Tolman, 1992; Shupe, Stacey, & Hazelwood, 1987).

Prospects for a New Model

Common Ground

There are several ways to address the differing perspectives and thus increase the potential for cooperation and more comprehensive intervention (see Figure 1.2). One is to begin to identify and recognize the common ground that already exists between the woman battering and the mental health fields. The mental health field, for instance, has helped develop our understanding of trauma, particularly posttraumatic stress, which helps explain the effects of woman battering (Herman, 1992). Clinical psychologists working with battered women have been at the forefront in critiquing conventional treatments and devising new ones (Browne, 1993; Dutton, 1992b; Koss et al., 1994; Walker, 1994). They have developed therapies for women that address the specific psychological effects associated with abuse and violence while tending to the safety and empowerment of battered women.

A second response to the differing perspectives might be to explore their complementary contributions. Most mental health approaches recognize the role of social factors in mental disorders and mental illness. Dysfunctional family structures and so-called social stressors may help initiate disorders and exacerbate them. Identifying and reducing stressors such as woman battering and abuse would no doubt increase the effectiveness of mental health treatment (Dutton, 1992b; Herman, 1992; Koss et al., 1994; Walker, 1994). Assessment and safety procedures developed by battered women's advocates would be helpful in this regard.

The mental health field has also done much to promote the beneficial role of social support in countering detrimental stressors and increasing the response to treatment (Herman, 1992). It has developed a rich literature on the procedures and dynamics of group counseling that builds this social support. Battered women's advocates have similarly identified social isolation as a common tactic and outcome of abuse, and the essential need for support groups to break that isolation and affirm a woman's strengths. Building social support for women may, therefore, be one place that mental health and battered women's services have common experience.

- Attention to trauma, particularly posttraumatic stress
- Recognition of the role of social factors in mental disorders
- The utility of social support in effective interventions
- The need for cost-saving linkages and referrals
- The emergence of a new, more holistic model of treatment

Figure 1.2. Common Ground for Battered Women's Programs and Mental Health Services

At an even more rudimentary level, each of the two fields offers the other services that can help extend their own work. Mental health services today are increasingly being pressured to develop more cost-effective outpatient services as a result of managed care and cost containment pressures in general. Similarly, the limited funding for community services, such as women's shelters and victim services, warrants their linking with services to expand their outreach. Battered women's programs can therefore offer mental health clinicians a vital referral source and a means to expand their limited scope.

Toward a New Model

Some clinicians-researchers claim that a new model is ultimately needed that integrates the two perspectives. Without such a model, the underlying conflicts and status differences may continue to cause problems. Training efforts and new protocols have had a limited effect on the identification of woman battering in mental health settings, perhaps for this reason (McLeer, Anwar, Herman, & Maquiling, 1989). According to an integrated model proposed by psychiatrist Carole Warshaw (1995a), the guiding premise would be that the majority of mental health symptoms in battered women are intricately linked to the abuse the women have received from men. The mental disorder is reinforced by social beliefs that condone abuse and the lack of resources that often help sustain the abuse. In other words, the traditional medical model needs to be expanded to include social context.

Such a model does not dismiss pathological symptoms, it reframes them as understandable responses to abuse. In addition, other disorders or symptomatology may actually be coping mechanisms or survival strategies used by battered women when healthier options are not available or effective. Being compliant, for example, may be a means of reducing a woman's immediate danger. If a woman does not feel there are viable options for leaving physically, she may attempt to change her situation by acting out emotionally—or disassociating herself from her feelings.

A step beyond reframing is implicit in the empowerment and survivor therapies and echoed in the alcoholic and children of alcoholics recovery movements (see Ackerman, 1987; Fossum, 1989). It envisions a more holistic response to family violence and dysfunction in general. This holistic perspective is based on spiritual presuppositions that individuals have strengths, resources, and spirit that often transcend desperate social circumstances. However vague or implicit, the empowerment and recovery movements acknowledge, affirm, and encourage the strength, courage, perseverance, ingenuity, and resiliency of battered women. These qualities shape the human spirit through a grace and healing of their own. They also prompt a person to seek help and make change, and in the process build a new sense of support and community (Peck, 1978, 1987).

■■ ORGANIZATIONAL BARRIERS

Identifying Barriers to Battered Women

To develop and implement a new approach to battered women, one must identify and counter organizational barriers. These barriers go beyond differences in professional approach, training, and experience. In fact, they often counteract the effect of new theoretical models, personal awareness, and innovative leadership. Organizational consultants and management analysts, therefore, attempt to assess such barriers in businesses or health services (Hammer & Stanton, 1993). They consider the actual experience of the customer or patient and what can be done to meet their objectives better. The result is often to revise staff-client interactions, modify staff responsibilities, and reorganize decision making. In a similar vein, this section identifies several of the organizational barriers facing battered women and poses some basic steps to counter them.

Inappropriate Treatment

The National Resource Center on Domestic Violence's survey of state domestic violence coalitions identified two major problems for battered women with regard to mental health services. One, the services provided for many battered women are inappropriate and even detrimental; two, the limited access to mental health services prevents many battered women from obtaining needed services (see Table 1.1). These two problems appear to reflect some underlying organizational barriers that ultimately need to be addressed to improve the experience of battered women in need of mental health services.

The most common problem identified by the coalitions is that mental health treatment is often considered inappropriate and even unacceptable for battered women. The vast majority of the states (80%) report mental health treatment is too often "dangerous," "useless," "detrimental," or "ineffective" to battered women. They complain of "victim-blaming," "misdiagnosis," "over-medication," "couples counseling," no accountability for the batterers, and little attention to safety. More fundamentally, the perception among the battered women's advocates is that mental health treatment, intentionally or not, tends to send the message that battered women are "sick," and by implication that they are at least in part to blame for their abuse.

A substantial portion of the advocates were also concerned about the lack of availability of mental health services. Half (50%) of the coalitions mentioned some difficulty in gaining access to services. Four major problems were mentioned repeatedly: the lack of services within communities, the prohibitive cost of services for women who have little or no income, the distance women have to travel to receive services, and the long waiting periods for women who need low-cost help. Forty percent of the respondents cited the cost of mental health services as one of the major barriers. A few coalitions also noted that psychiatric facilities occasionally dump women into battered women's shelters when their insurance runs out, with little regard for the additional mental health care they need. Furthermore, little specialized mental health care is available for children, who experience significant distress from witnessing violence and whose mothers are suffering from serious emotional problems.

In essence, the mental health services do not seem well suited for the situation of many battered women, especially those in contact with battered women's shelters. These women tend to be in a state of crisis or transition that makes it difficult for them to seek out mental health services and to sustain contact when they reach a suitable service. These women often have little income, lack transportation, and have the re-

Evaluation Process

- DSM-IV diagnosis and case disposition
- Clinical questioning that limits social context or analysis
- Institutional constraints
- Insurance reimbursement/ability to pay
- Woman abuse as a social work or criminal problem
- Social control and labeling of clients or patients

Professional Training

- Professional socialization to focus on pathology
- Personal discomfort or insecurity in dealing with abuse
- Professional hierarchy that resists paraprofessional experience

Figure 1.3. Organizational Barriers in Mental Health Settings

sponsibility of children. They additionally face decreasing services for low-income people and cuts in funding that would subsidize their payments to such services.

The problems of battered women, noted by the surveyed advocates, also imply organizational barriers within mental health services that might be addressed. One such organizational barrier is the evaluation procedures that appear to contribute to the inappropriate treatment and diagnosis cited by the advocates. Another organizational barrier is that some mental health services do not readily accommodate or reach out to battered women. Some battered women, according to some advocates and researchers, may be retraumatized by the professional status of mental health clinicians once they do contact services.

The Evaluation Process

Research in the field termed *medical sociology* has extensively examined the organizational barriers to appropriate assessment and treatment in health services generally (e.g., Anspach, 1988; Fisher, 1986; Kurz, 1987; Mishler, 1984; Waitzkin, 1989). Researchers have identified several barriers that include the evaluation process, professional training, and institutional constraints (see Figure 1.3). Those specifically studying the response to battered women have found similar problems that need to be addressed (Gondolf, 1990).

Researchers have most thoroughly observed and analyzed the so-called discourse of the evaluation process (e.g., Anspach, 1988; Kuipers, 1989). The structure of evaluation questioning appears to negate the social world or real-life experiences of many clients. Clinicians tend to ask close-ended questions that focus on symptoms related to physical and psychological disorders. They tend to interrupt, question, or ignore additional information that has to do with relationships, abuse, economic problems, and so on. In research of a psychiatric emergency room, for instance, few clinicians asked follow-up questions to patients' reports of violence and abuse (Gondolf, 1992). As discussed in Chapter 3, "Case Studies of Mental Health Evaluations," clinicians are likely to minimize the violence in clinical reports, listing it as one of many social issues, describing it as a secondary symptom of the mental disorder, or redefining it as an inconsequential conflict (e.g., woman battering becomes "marital dispute").

The predominant explanation for this apparent neglect of abuse and battering is that the intent of mental health evaluation precludes it (Waitzkin, 1989). The primary objective of most evaluations is to establish a psychiatric diagnosis and prescribe the corresponding treatment. This objective is reinforced and rewarded by comments and criticisms in staff meetings, insurance reimbursements, and training procedures and protocols. According to researchers, the interactions among clinicians in a mental health setting amount to an ongoing socialization process that further "teaches" clinicians to keep focused on mental diagnosis and prescribed treatment.

Institutional constraints affect the evaluation and assessment process. The client's ability to pay, the availability of beds, open appointments, or group openings can influence the extent and nature of triage. The priority of evaluation admittedly shifts in many services to whether the client should be accepted into one of the limited treatment openings. If the clients can pay, have a treatable disorder, and appear fairly compliant, they are more likely to get in (Lidz & Mulvey, 1990). Clinicians, more practically, often claim they simply do not have enough time to assess all that they should, and do not have the expertise to do so. They are charged with screening for an increasing variety of problems, depression and suicide, dangerousness and lethality, eating disorders and substance abuse, AIDS and other sexually transmitted diseases, as well as child abuse and woman battering.

- Difficult access and high costs limit quality care
- Professional status retraumatizes many abused women
- Treatment replicates dynamics of abuse
- Safety issues are not adequately addressed
- Couples interviewing and counseling endanger women
- Misdiagnoses and inappropriate diagnoses
- Diagnosis detrimental in custody and divorce cases

Figure 1.4. Consequences of Organizational Barriers

There are other explanations as well. The professional role assumed by many mental health clinicians often distances them from their client's social world (Fisher, 1986; Warshaw, 1993). They are trained to treat identified mental disorders and problems. Understandably, some feel powerless or inadequate before the complicated and unsettling social issues compounding their clients' lives. Some clinicians may as well feel personal discomfort in response to reported abuse that touches on similar problems in their own lives. A high proportion of mental health clinicians have experienced abuse in their own families. Many have also, in a sense, encountered an abusive situation in their training. They were isolated from friends and family, forced to devalue other parts of themselves, and had their own self-esteem diminished (Warshaw, 1989).

Professional Status

The professional training of clinicians also translates into a professional status that raises problems for some battered women (Sugg & Inui, 1992; Warshaw, 1993). *Professional status* refers to the authority, specialized knowledge, and routine procedures often associated with certified mental health staff. Some battered women are retraumatized in mental health services as a result of their interactions with those who appear as professionals (see Figure 1.4). There are several ways in which the retraumatization (or reexperiencing the abuse) may occur. For one, battered women in mental health services may encounter psychologists or psychiatrists who exercise extreme authority. As a result, battered women often reexperience dynamics similar to those with their abusive partner who exerted authority and dominance over them. Moreover, they are likely to be directed, scrutinized, and interrogated by male staff in a way reminiscent of their controlling abusers, who typically order and watch over them.[2]

A second problem is that battered women may feel uneasy about speaking to male professionals about personal issues associated with their abuse. They often appear confused, fearful, disoriented, and pessimistic in response to their abuse (Dutton, 1992b), and may therefore not be entirely consistent or coherent during an evaluation interview. Consequently, some battered women may appear "noncompliant" or "resistant," and as a result are treated sternly or even harshly, subjected to strict regimens, or involuntarily committed to inpatient care. They may also be labeled with a detrimental diagnosis or characterized negatively in clinical records.

A third source of retraumatization may be the nature of inpatient or hospital treatment that professionals prescribe (Warshaw, 1993). Hospitalization usually restricts a woman's movement and puts a battered woman under surveillance—the same kind of control that her abusive partner subjects her to. She often has to forfeit personal items, clothing, and familiar surroundings, which further attacks her sense of identity—an identity already systematically degraded by many abusers. Additionally, medication may confirm the claims of an abusive partner that the woman has to change, that there is something "wrong" with her, as the abuser often claims as one of his tactics of control.

Woman Battering Protocol

The organizational barriers to responding appropriately to battered women may be eased with a more accommodating perspective. If the barriers are largely a manifestation of the underlying medical model, as some researchers suggest, a change in outlook is liable to bring a change in mental health procedures and structures. Innovative programs addressing women's medical issues are emerging in response to new conceptions of gender and health, and procedures for evaluating and assessing women have dramatically changed in recent years as a result of a general awareness of women's unique needs (e.g., Caplan, 1985; Herman, 1992; Rieker & Carmen, 1984). But even without a dramatic overhaul of the medical model, substantial procedural and institutional changes can be made that will benefit battered women.

Probably the greatest advances have been toward revised screening and assessment protocols (Dutton, 1992b; Gondolf, 1990; Schechter, 1987;

- *Screening questions* that specifically ask about aspects of abuse
- *Abuse history inventory* that establishes nature, duration, frequency, and effect
- *Clinical records* that explicitly describe the abuse and its primary importance
- *Diagnosis* that accounts for abuse history and diagnostic consequences, e.g., PTSD
- *Safety plan* that outlines steps to escape violence, assure protection, and obtain help and support
- *Lethality assessment* that assists woman in a realistic determination of risk and dangerousness

---

Figure 1.5. Woman Battering Protocol

Warshaw, 1995b). These protocols systematically examine the likelihood that an individual has been abused, the dynamics and history of that abuse, the effects and trauma caused by that abuse, the safety measures and protection available to avoid further abuse and violence, and detailed documentation of the abuse in clinical records (see Figure 1.5). Such procedures can do much to increase the identification of woman abuse and initiate supportive assistance to battered women, as discussed in Chapter 4, "Procedures for Assessing Woman Battering."

Evaluations of training and protocols for woman battering suggest that more needs to be done, however. The introduction of protocols in medical settings does increase identification of woman battering in the short run, but institutional barriers tend to reverse the progress in time (McLeer et al., 1989). Staff turnover, professional socialization, and institutional constraints all take their toll. Consequently, structural and organizational changes need to accompany the introduction of protocols for them to endure. Several of these innovations are discussed in Chapter 2, "Moving Toward Collaboration."

These kinds of support usually require a tremendous amount of groundwork. Substantial change in protocol and institutional practices, in fact, typically results from a long-term exchange between battered women's programs and mental health services. A place to start is by acknowledging the different perspectives and related organizational barriers and the need to broaden the scope of mental health services to serve battered women better.

■ CONCLUSION

This chapter has examined the fundamental differences in perspective between battered women's advocates and mental health clinicians and the organizational barriers that confront battered women in need of mental health services. Prevailing assumptions in the mental health field, represented in the medical model, emphasize the role of individual psychopathology or a dysfunctional family system in abusive relationships. This compares to the focus on social factors that typifies the battered women's movement. At the same time, some common ground is emerging that forms the basis of increased cooperation and collaboration between the respective fields. Both battered women's programs and mental health services share an attention to trauma and posttraumatic stress, the role of social factors in mental disorders, the use of social support in effective intervention, and the need for cost-saving linkages and referrals. There are also prospects for a new model that integrates assumptions from both fields in a more holistic response to family problems in general.

Some immediate, practical steps may be taken to offset, at least to some degree, organizational barriers. The most fundamental is the implementation of a revised screening and assessment protocol that specifically addresses woman battering. This kind of protocol has been shown to increase identification of the violence many women endure. Several organizational innovations (such as protocol monitoring, on-site women's advocates, and training sessions) can help maintain revised protocols amid frequent staff turnover and other pressing demands in mental health settings. A sustained exchange between battered women's advocates and mental health clinicians is needed to build the trust, familiarity, and understanding that make such innovations happen.

■ NOTES

1. There is significant variation in approach and perspective among mental health clinicians. Those trained as social workers are especially more likely to ascribe to a broader sociological perspective or human ecological model that emphasizes the influence of one's social environment and culture on behavior. Similarly, clinicians trained in social psychology or systems theory are more likely to attend to the role of social norms and structure in one's behavior.

2. These problems were forcefully raised at a conference focusing on women, abuse, and mental health services titled "Dare to Vision," convened in Washington, D.C., by the Center for Mental Health Services and the Human Resource Center of the Northeast (Center for Mental Health Services, 1995). Representatives from organizations such as the National Empowerment Center and the Alliance for the Mentally Ill, along with battered women's advocates and mental health clinicians working with battered women, offered case studies and analyses of consequences for conventional mental health treatment on women in general.

2

Moving Toward Collaboration

Improving the assessment of battered women is more than a matter of new information, new tools, and new procedures. At the same time, it does not mean a disruptive and imposing change in mental health services. Some level of cooperation between mental health services and battered women's services is needed to help implement and sustain a woman battering protocol and to create new joint services and referral sources for battered women. Cooperation may entail, at one level, an exchange of information, referrals, and consultation. More substantial collaboration may be warranted, however, to address the perspective and structural obstacles raised in Chapter 1, " Addressing Differences and Barriers."

This chapter explores how clinicians and advocates might move toward new models of collaboration. It outlines what specifically might be done in mental health settings to implement revisions in assessment protocol to respond to battered women more appropriately. First, a survey of state coalitions for battered women's programs is reviewed to show the current level of cooperation. Examples of more extensive cooperation and collaboration in other fields are discussed to illustrate further possibilities for the mental health and woman battering fields.

Finally, specific steps are outlined to establish this sort of collaboration and, minimally, to sustain the implementation of a woman battering protocol. I first discuss the individual initiative and implementation aids that might be used to put a woman battering protocol in place. I then consider the institutional supports and program linkages that help sustain protocol changes, improve service delivery, and build new possibilities. The steps together suggest a process of collaboration that serves as a catalyst for change, as well as a support for it.

■■ EXISTING COOPERATION

Referral and Case Consultation

The survey of state coalitions for battered women's programs provides some indication of the nature of existing cooperation among battered women's programs and mental health services (see the appendix). It also suggests possible directions for more extensive cooperation that may develop into a more genuinely collaborative effort. Women's programs and mental health services do make occasional referrals to one another and consult with one another on special cases.

As indicated in Table 2.1, the vast majority of the programs refer battered women to mental health professionals (80%) and maintain a list of mental health professionals for this purpose (78%). About two thirds (64%) of the women's programs consult with mental health professionals about women clients, but few (4%) act as paid consultants to mental health agencies or assist with psychiatric commitment hearings (5%). About half of the shelters are already involved in some form of training: An estimated 45% of the battered women's programs train mental health staff, and 54% advise mental health services on woman battering protocols. More substantial affiliations for cosponsoring training conferences have been established by less than one fifth (17%) of the programs.

The state coalitions reported receiving a variety of assistance from mental health services, primarily in the form of referrals and consultations. Over half of the women's programs have received direct assistance from mental health professionals, as shown in Table 2.2. For instance, 56% have obtained mental health counseling for individual women, and 66% have received referrals from mental health professionals. Approximately one third of the women's programs have received

TABLE 2.1 Battered Women's Programs Initiating Mental Health
Cooperation

80%	Refer individual women for mental health therapy or counseling with a licensed professional or mental health agency staff.
64%	Consult with mental health professionals about individual women clients.
27%	Consult with mental health professionals about individual batterers.
49%	Provide shelter to women with psychiatric problems and coordinate work with mental health agencies.
78%	Maintain a referral list of therapists appropriate for battered women.
27%	Maintain a list of therapists who work as expert witnesses.
4%	Work as paid consultants to mental health agencies.
45%	Train mental health staff about woman battering.
17%	Cosponsor training conferences with mental health agencies.
54%	Advise mental health agencies about woman battering protocols.
10%	Design woman battering policies and procedures for mental health agencies.
5%	Testify at women's commitment hearings to psychiatric hospitals.
2%	Testify at batterers' commitment hearings to psychiatric hospitals.

Other types of collaborations:

Other Responses	# of States Responding	Percentage of States
Referrals for related services	4	13
Jointly run programs	4	13
Joint training	3	10
Task force/study groups	3	10
Cooperative consultations	3	10
Boards with MH and WB members	2	6

NOTE: n = 896 battered women's programs (based on estimates from 30 states'
domestic violence coalitions responding to survey)
MH = Mental health; WB = Woman battering

assistance in the form of emergency psychiatric consultation (34%), shelter training on psychiatric issues (27%), or representation on shelter boards (31%). Only 1 in 10 (11%) of the states (29 reporting) have any standards or guidelines for mental health professionals on woman battering, however. The existing guidelines are primarily for certification of

TABLE 2.2 Battered Women's Programs Receiving Mental Health Services

56%	Offer individual counseling to abused women.
66%	Refer battered women to shelters and battered women's support groups.
14%	Offer groups for children who have witnessed woman battering.
43%	Provide individual counseling to batterers.
22%	Provide counseling groups for batterers.
34%	Offer emergency psychiatric consultation to shelter staff.
27%	Train shelter staff about psychiatric issues or substance abuse management.
31%	Have mental health agency staff serving as board members of shelter.

Other types of services:

Other Responses	# of States Responding	Percentage of States
Work jointly with clients	8	27
Coeducation/cotraining	4	13
WB crisis intervention	3	10
Assessment for WB	3	10

NOTE: n = 896 battered women's programs (based on estimates from 30 states' domestic violence coalitions responding to survey)
MH = Mental health; WB = Woman battering

woman battering and sexual assault programs, rather than to direct mental health services and individual professionals in their treatment of battered women.

Improving Cooperation

The survey also helped identify the positive tools and innovations that advance cooperation between the two fields. The suggestions emphasized the need for more training, task groups, and joint projects (see Table 2.3). The call, overall, was for battered women's advocates and mental health clinicians to do more together, and in the process communicate more directly with one another about common concerns and issues. Several concrete examples that have been tried are worth noting:

TABLE 2.3 Innovations to Improve Collaboration

Response	# of States Responding	Percentage of States
Training	13	43
Task force or study group	10	33
More communication	10	33
Joint projects	5	17
Conferences	4	13
MH and WB serve together on a board	4	13

NOTE: 24 States responded; $n = 30$
MH = Mental health; WB = Woman battering

- An annual breakfast sponsored by battered women's programs for substance abuse, mental health, and family counselors
- A multidisciplinary task group addressing problematic child abuse cases
- A conference series on health and wellness for battered women's advocates and mental health and substance abuse practitioners
- A "point person" at the mental health center to handle questions, problems, and concerns of battered women's advocates
- A support group run by battered women's advocates at a local mental health center, and mental health clinicians providing a group therapy session in a local shelter
- Monthly meetings with the state division of mental health to discuss the relationship between battered women's services and mental health centers and the needs for program development in this area
- An annual statewide training conference on mental health, substance abuse, and domestic violence organized by an interagency committee
- Woman battering presentations to graduate psychology classes and placement of psychology students in the women's programs

With the exception of three or four states, most of these innovations are locally based and maintained by the efforts of a few key people. Few statewide public policy, training programs, or clearing houses are underway, and joint ventures between state domestic violence coalitions and mental health associations or professional societies are, at this stage, minimal.

■■ EXAMPLES OF COLLABORATION

The barriers between the battered women's programs and mental health services might seem to preclude possibilities for further collaboration. Not only different perspectives but also different levels of status may limit a genuine partnership in which representatives from both fields contribute on an equal basis (Gondolf, 1990; Stark & Flitcraft, 1996). As suggested in Chapter 1, "Addressing Differences and Barriers," many battered women's advocates are not confident that their expertise can be heard, accepted, or used in many mental health settings given the implicit imbalance of status between the two fields. The professional status of mental health clinicians is reinforced by credentialing, third-party billing, professional associations, substantial salaries, and community deference, whereas advocates have historically received much less formal recognition, reimbursement, or esteem as workers in a community-based service.

Some useful examples of dialogue and innovation, even among unmatched factions, suggest that substantial collaboration is still possible. The community mental health movement and the advent of Alcoholics Anonymous (AA), for instance, illustrate ways in which collaboration was established despite formidable barriers and differences. Organizational innovations and new policies emerged that supported and sustained joint responses to individuals' problems. The collaborations were born largely out of community-based groups that raised concerns, established professionals who reached out to other groups and organizations, and community workers who posed practical and beneficial innovations.

The Community Mental Health Movement

The community mental health movement, which accompanied the deinstitutionalization of the 1960s, began with a public health model of intervention (Caplan, 1964). From this framework, both psychiatrists and psychologists attempted to integrate themselves more directly into the community. The idea was to treat the community as a patient, furthering a healthy environment and thus helping to prevent mental illness at its social roots. Professionals worked closely with self-help groups, local support groups, and group homes not only to address the symptoms of patients, but also to help improve their living situations.

One vestige of this movement is the community mental health centers (CMHCs) that remain the primary source of outpatient referral. In fact, the majority of patients evaluated in a psychiatric hospital are referred to CMHCs, as are most all discharged inpatients. Most of the current CMHCs operate under what might be considered a medical model rather than the more ecological or community-action model of their founding. The initial effort to bring the community concerns into the field of psychiatry has been supplanted, for the most part, by an extension of the hospital into the community (Dunham, 1976). Nevertheless, a precedent of community involvement and an organizational structure for collaboration remain.

Alcoholics Anonymous

Another example of collaboration is of a grassroots movement that now openly cooperates with conventional health services. AA was founded in direct opposition to the medical practices of the 1930s. Alcoholism, to the founding AA members, has a social dimension that hospital care overlooks. It takes tremendous social support and spiritual renewal to offset the physical addiction of alcoholism and to counter the social pressures and societal norms that encourage a return to drinking. Heavy drinking, in this light, is more than a psychiatric or emotional problem (Denzin, 1987).

Although there is still tension between the self-help approach of AA and hospital treatment, there is a stalwart cooperation as well. Many hospitals refer patients directly to an AA program after inpatient detoxi-fication and rehabilitation treatment. Some hospitals actually have AA meetings convening in the hospital; this brings additional programming to the inpatients and helps ease their transition back into the community. Many hospital-based alcohol programs incorporate AA principles into their own psychotherapy and support groups.

There are, of course, limits to such an example; AA has been domi-nated by white middle-class men preoccupied with their own personal recovery and often neglectful of its members' abuse of women. Battered women's advocates have criticized AA for its contradictory conception of powerless alcoholics and for misuses of "making amends" with one's partner (Frank & Kadison, 1992; Kasl, 1992; Tallen; 1990). Nevertheless, AA shows that a grassroots group with a fundamentally social analysis can build bridges with the medical establishment.

■■ TOWARD COLLABORATION

Collaboration between battered women's advocates and mental health clinicians on the order of the above examples is on the increase. In the meantime, some immediate steps can help build collaboration. These steps might center on establishing and maintaining more appropriate assessment of battered women in mental health settings. (Part II, "Tools for Improved Assessment," presents tools and procedures for assessing woman battering that make up a woman battering protocol.) As suggested in Chapter 1, "Addressing Differences and Barriers," implementing a protocol for woman battering may circumvent some of the structural barriers and help precipitate more cooperation. Identifying woman battering will help substantiate the need for more thorough assessment. The assessment is likely to necessitate more training and consultation with advocates. The assessments will also identify cases that would benefit from referral to battered women services, as well as from joint treatments or interventions.

To establish and maintain a woman battering protocol requires a supportive environment and a collaboration among battered women's services and mental health programs. Woman battering training and protocol tend to be compromised in most medical settings by staff turnover, procedural inertia, other clinical priorities, and institutional constraints (Gondolf, 1990; McLeer et al., 1989; Warshaw, 1993). Some accessible aids can help implement a woman battering protocol within a mental health setting, and some interpersonal actions can help sustain it. Additionally, institutional supports and community linkages are an essential part in sustaining protocol and acting on it (Browne, 1993; Gondolf, 1990; Warshaw, 1995b).

The successful assessment of battered women in mental health services is the manifestation of collaboration between advocates and clinicians. It is the result of not only the availability of tools and procedures but also individual initiatives, institutional supports, and program linkages. The broader collaboration process is a program, institutional, and community development process. Although the strategy for such development is likely to vary among different communities and different programs, a few basic ingredients are essential: individual initiatives, implementation aids, institutional supports, and program linkages. The chronological order and prominence of these ingredients may also vary, but precedent in other fields suggests that some attention to these ingredients is necessary if change is to be beneficial and enduring.

Individual Initiatives

Most collaborations are built on the initiatives of a few committed and forward-looking individuals who are willing to take the first steps beyond their immediate responsibilities to explore some new possibilities. These steps can be as simple as raising assessment issues with coworkers and conferring with other agencies and services about woman battering (see Figure 2.1). Casual conversations about others' observations on woman battering can approximate an informal survey of who is interested in the issue, as well as raise interest in it.

Interested staff might test some available tools and procedures, such as those presented in Chapter 5, "Recognizing the Strengths of Battered Women," and collect pilot data on the number and characteristics of battered women identified by the tools. This experience and data can help substantiate an otherwise personal concern into an institutional issue worthy of administrators' attention and support. At this point, administrators might grant some time and funds to obtain training and materials, or interested staff might simply develop contacts with a network of battered women's advocates at the local and state levels for further suggestions, advice, information, and support. This network might produce speakers or materials that could elaborate the opportunities to administrators or other staff.

Many battered women's programs offer basic training on battering issues for agencies in their community at little or no charge. Contact with representatives from battered women's programs can also help in developing a list of referrals and consultation sources necessary in formulating treatment plans and recommendations for assessed battered women. Often other mental health services, drug and alcohol programs, or child services are dealing with woman battering as well. Contacting them might reveal additional support and referral sources and some useful innovations that might be adopted at one's own agency.

Raising Awareness

- Identify interested staff or staff already versed in assessing woman battering
- Discuss with colleagues and administrators opportunities for and obstacles to appropriate assessment
- Use pilot instruments to identify implementation issues
- Collect pilot data of number of battered women and their characteristics
- Obtain allocation of time and support from administration for the need demonstrated in pilot data

Obtaining Information

- Find out about available battered women's services and legal provisions in the community for consultation and referral
- Confer with battered women's services about available trainers and materials
- Contact domestic violence coalitions, task groups, and organizations at the state level for additional information and advice
- Identify other mental health services, substance abuse programs, or general hospitals in the community that are addressing woman battering

Figure 2.1. Personal Initiatives for Establishing a Woman Battering Protocol

For example, a substance abuse counselor at a veterans' hospital substance abuse unit initiated some dramatic program changes through similar personal initiatives (see Foster & Gondolf, 1989). He began to ask coworkers about the battering that occasionally was suggested by his clients. The coworkers noted similar indications of battering in some of their cases and were curious about them. The counselor and a coworker began to phone woman battering programs in their region and around the country to find out more about what was being done and how to do it. The counselor then arranged to administer a battering inventory to a group of patients and found that the reporting on the inventory was nearly 10 times that reported in clinical records. The inventory data and program information were presented to administrators and led to training and the establishment of a woman battering treatment program within the substance abuse unit. The counselor sought out several responsive advocates to act as consultants and collaborators. With their

Staff Reminders

- Protocol forms and outlines included in intake packets, forms, and/or files
- Reminder forms or checklists to encourage routine assessment of woman battering
- Referral and consultation lists put in all clinical sites
- Posters placed in clinical areas that outline what to ask and what to do to identify and assess woman battering

Environmental Supports

- Articles, manuals, and booklets with more in-depth information made readily available to staff
- Videos to increase understanding of women's abuse experiences and therapeutic techniques for dealing with them made part of inservice trainings or staff meetings
- Visible supports for women: waiting-room brochures, wallet-size information cards, posted emergency phone numbers, wall posters on woman battering, and reading materials on battering

Figure 2.2. Implementation Aids to Woman Battering Protocol

outside help and inside administrative support, the program received substantial funding for what was considered to be a new and creative initiative.

Implementation Aids

Establishing a protocol for identifying and assessing woman battering offers a "doable" goal that may act as a catalyst for broader objectives. The challenge is how to implement such a protocol amid the institutional constraints and program inertia that often counter the best intentions and most sophisticated techniques. Conversations with coworkers about the procedures and obstacles at a particular mental health setting should illuminate areas that need special attention and creative response. Several aids have been developed for promoting the implementation of woman battering assessment in hospital emergency rooms (Warshaw, 1995b). These suggest some of the simple things that can be devised to promote the implementation of such a protocol in other mental health services (see Figure 2.2).

One kind of aid is systematic reminders for staff to identify and assess woman battering. Outlines or checklists of a woman battering protocol might be included in in-take packets, be attached to in-take forms, or enclosed in clinical files. A list of response procedures, referral sources, and consultants might be posted in interview offices. A second set of aids focuses on creating a supportive environment—that is, a place where greater visible attention is given to woman battering in general. The support might first come through the knowledge and understanding of the staff. A variety of materials is available to inform staff about the nature of abuse and services to deal with it; many of these may be obtained from local, state, or national organizations devoted to addressing woman battering. Several clinical and research articles are available as well that provide an overview of knowledge in the field. Some of these are listed in the bibliography at the end of this book. The National Resource Center on Domestic Violence (1-800-537-2238) also provides materials and references. Several training and information videos are available through many battered women's programs or university libraries.

The growing awareness and commitment of clinicians might be communicated through some visible supports for women. Brochures about woman battering in the waiting room, emergency phone numbers posted in women's restrooms or on vestibule bulletin boards, and features in newsletters about women and abuse help reinforce the importance of disclosing battering and taking action to counter it. The Family Violence Prevention Fund is leading a national campaign against domestic violence that adds several engaging wall posters on the subject to others already available through women's shelters and state coalitions. Some services have developed wallet-sized information cards for clinicians to present to women or have reading materials, such as *When Love Goes Wrong: What to Do When You Can't Do Anything Right* by Ann Jones and Susan Schechter (1992), available for interested clients. It may be wise to have a battered woman read the materials at the agency rather than take them home, because a battering man may use them against her if he sees them.

Institutional Support

An additional level of action generally needs to be attained if a woman battering protocol is to be sustained over time amid the obstacles that so often counter organizational changes. Mechanisms need to be in

Monitoring and Reviews

- Discussion of abuse and battering case presentations and clinical conferences
- Protocol monitoring by administrative or supervisory staff
- Periodic review of assessment procedures and outcome of cases

Retraining and Evaluation

- Woman battering as a routine part of educational structure of the institutions (staff orientations, inservice training, rounds)
- Periodic follow-up training on assessing woman battering for all clinicians and staff
- Data collection on the number of identified cases and their characteristics
- Institutional research on the implementation, utility, and effectiveness of battering assessment:

  Have clinician knowledge, attitude, and use of assessment tools improved?

  Have the treatment plans and referrals been consistent with the assessments?

  Have the assessments improved the safety and well-being of the assessed women?

Figure 2.3. Institutional Supports for Sustaining Woman Battering Protocol

place that routinely monitor and review assessment procedures without relying on individual personalities, good intentions, or professional habits. They need to approximate a set of systemic checks and balances against the ebb and flow of personnel, training, interest, and priorities (see Figure 2.3).

One kind of support might be protocol monitoring and review. For instance, clinicians might be expected to discuss abuse and battering in case presentations and clinical conferences and to be questioned by accompanying staff if the topic is overlooked. Reporting on abuse might, in this way, become as routine as presenting the prospects of suicide or self-care in a mental health meeting. Supervisory staff might periodically observe in-takes, assessments, and records to see that a woman battering protocol is being implemented and to look for ways to revise and improve it.

Another kind of institutional support to help sustain protocol is retraining and evaluation. The topic of woman battering might be made an ongoing part of the educational structure of a mental health agency or service. It might be reviewed as a part of staff orientations, internships, in-service training, or hospital rounds. Periodic follow-up training on assessment of woman battering is also needed to inform new staff and ensure consistent implementation among existing staff. All staff need occasional retraining to address the increasingly complex demands of today's mental health services and the distraction they sometimes present.

Finally, some means to evaluate the implementation, utility, and effectiveness of battering assessments is needed to determine the direction of training and procedures more objectively. At a minimum, a staff person can periodically review records to determine the number of identified cases and their characteristics.

- Is the number of cases remaining fairly constant?
- Are they similar in characteristics? If not, why not?
- Has the kind of client notably changed, or is the battering protocol less vigorously invoked?

More elaborate institutional research might also be pursued to address questions about the effectiveness of such assessment:

- Have clinicians' knowledge, attitude, and use of assessment tools improved?
- Have the treatment plans and referrals been consistent with the assessments?
- Have the assessments improved the safety and well-being of the assessed battered women?

This level of evaluation, of course, requires more of a commitment of resources and research expertise. Ideally, surveys, questionnaires, and interviews are constructed, administered, and analyzed by trained researchers. Program evaluation of this sort is, nonetheless, increasingly expected and even required by funders, and therefore may warrant funding as a line item in project grants and program budgets.

Program Linkages

Formal linkages between battered women's programs and mental health services need to be established to ensure an exchange of information and expertise. A woman battering protocol is more likely to take

Service Links

- Monthly lunch-time discussion, case consultation, or task group with battered women's advocates
- On-site advocates with specialized training to assist identified battered women (similar to presence in courtrooms)
- Specialized groups for battered women led by advocates meeting at mental health service

Development Links

- Pursuit of earmarked funding for cross-training, joint projects, and new model programs
- An ongoing work group of mental health clinicians, battered women's advocates, and representatives from other agencies addressing woman battering (police, substance abuse programs, child protection services, neighborhood development groups)
- State guidelines or standards to ensure priority of protocol (similar to suicide or child abuse guidelines)
- Curriculum changes at clinical psychology programs, social work schools, and medical schools to ensure instruction in battered women's issues

Figure 2.4. Program Linkages to Enhance Woman Battering Protocol

hold amid knowledge of its necessity and utility (Gondolf, 1990; Jacobson, Koehler, & Jones-Brown, 1987; McLeer et al., 1989; Rose & Saunders, 1986). Moreover, linkages that formally tie advocates and clinicians form the basis for genuine collaboration and innovation. External reinforcement for institutional supports and new joint projects is more likely to emerge. For instance, joint treatment programs for battered women with chronic mental disorders have been developed through some formal linkages (see Figure 2.4).

The notion of linkages might take several different forms. First, service linkages institute formal exchanges between advocates and clinicians for improving assessment and treatment. Advocates and clinicians might be scheduled to meet monthly for lunch-time discussions about problematic cases, service delivery, or policy issues, such as reporting or warning requirements. Advocates might be assigned to serve in mental health settings much as they have in the courts. They could be available in mental health clinics or psychiatric emergency rooms to conduct in-depth assessments and safety planning with women who have been screened as likely to have been abused or battered. The advocates would help ease the additional workload of clinicians and ensure that expertise about woman battering is readily available. Advocates might also lead or assist in specialized groups at mental health services for battered women diagnosed with mental problems.

Linkages for the purpose of developing the mental health contribution to addressing woman battering should also be considered. Clinicians, advocates, and representatives from other agencies are increasingly forming task groups to explore ways to establish more comprehensive service interventions. They are attempting to devise approaches that will not only increase effectiveness but also increase efficiency. Shared or joint services can often improve delivery and save money by not creating overlapping or duplicate programs. In the process, the parties involved learn more about each others' programs and expertise. This in itself can lead to more probing assessments and more frequent referrals.

Finally, collaborative task groups might work toward improving state mental health guidelines to ensure the appropriate assessment of battered women, much as has been done with regard to child abuse, suicide, and "harm to others." As part of state and national professional associations, such groups might also work to change curriculum in clinical psychology programs, social work schools, and training hospitals to include specific instruction in battered women's issues. In this way, the awareness and knowledge of woman battering might become a fact of professional practice.

■ CONCLUSION

Existing cooperation between battered women's programs and mental services appears to be primarily in the form of occasional referrals and consultations. According to our survey, many advocates and clinicians are urging and even attempting more substantial exchanges through cross-training and joint projects, however. There is evidence from other fields that cooperation of this sort might eventually grow into collaboration despite imbalances in professional status and the prevailing differences in perspective. The relationship between recovery groups such as AA and treatment hospitals provides such an example.

The steps in building this kind of collaboration might be applied to implementing and sustaining the assessment of battered women in mental health settings. Individual initiative, such as identifying interested or concerned coworkers, might be used to introduce a woman battering protocol and test it out. Various implementation aids, such as protocol checklists and waiting-room brochures, might serve as reminders to busy staff and as support to women clients. Regular monitoring, review, and formal evaluation of the protocol represent the kind of institutional supports that sustain appropriate assessment. Finally, program linkages are essential to building an ongoing exchange of information that can spark joint projects, additional referrals, and new policies.

Collaboration of this kind is a development process that creates a climate for improved assessment and a means of creating new possibilities that go beyond differences and barriers.

PART II

Tools for
Improved Assessment

3

Case Studies of Mental Health Evaluations

Mental Health Evaluation

In this chapter, I take an extended look at the mental health evaluation of battered women to assess the concerns of battered women's advocates and the challenges that face mental health clinicians. The cases illustrate the differences in perspective and approach between mental health clinicians and advocates and suggest the practical issues that face professionals in both specialties. The cases suggest that identifying psychiatric symptomatology often takes precedence over assessing the dangers commonly associated with woman battering.

I summarize the mental health evaluations of three battered women and analyze them from the differing perspectives of battered women's advocates and mental health clinicians. The first case is that of a woman whose abusive husband has her committed to a psychiatric hospital because of her doing "weird things," including recently threatening suicide. The second case is that of a woman with a long history of being abused who went to a psychiatric hospital seeking help in a custody battle with her abusive husband. The third case is that of a battered woman sent to a psychiatric hospital after suffering from an overdose of drugs. None of the patients was referred to battered women's services or presented with safety procedures such as calling the police or friends for protection.[1]

Source and Context of the Cases

The cases presented in this chapter are drawn from a study of the evaluations and records of 382 psychiatric patients sponsored by the National Institute of Mental Health (Gondolf, 1990).[2] The sample represents patients who appeared in the emergency room of a metropolitan psychiatric hospital over a 6-month period. More than half the patients (57%) were male, two thirds (65%) were white, and the majority (80%) were not employed. The case information is drawn from near-verbatim transcripts of evaluation interviews and related staff meetings compiled by research observers trained in speed writing. In the evaluation process at the psychiatric hospital, a nurse-clinician first receives and interviews the patient. The clinician presents a brief summary of the case to the psychiatrist in a private meeting, and the psychiatrist then meets and interviews the patient to formulate the diagnoses and disposition of the case.

Only 8% of the total sample (32 cases out of 382) reported being the primary victim of some form of violence. Half of the self-identified victims (16 cases out of 32) in the emergency room were females assaulted by their spouses or partners and might be considered battered women. The victimization rate appears to represent a gross underreporting, however, given that other studies of psychiatric patients found as much as 10 times that rate of victimization (e.g., Carmen, Riecker, & Mills, 1984; Jacobson et al., 1987). Although I can only speculate on the patients' reluctance to report victimization, I did examine the psychiatric evaluation process for features that may contribute to the low rate of reported victimization.

Two main features were apparent deterrents to reporting. One, the majority of victims introduced the violence on their own initiative as part of the presenting problem (50%) or tangentially to unrelated questions (16%). The relatively few direct questions (only in 19% of the cases) about victimization were generally in response to information offered by individuals accompanying the patient to the emergency room or to some other cues that victimization had occurred. The absence of any routine inquiry about abuse or battering would seem to lessen the chances of women disclosing their being victimized.

Two, the disclosed victimization was not aggressively pursued by the clinician. Clinicians tended to follow up the patient's presentation of victimization with questions about the duration ("How long has this been going on?") or temporality ("When did the incident occur?"). There was little exploration of the nature, tactics, and circumstances, especially by psychiatrists. Other controlling behaviors often related to victimization were not explored. The full scope of victimization was likely to be overlooked in this sort of process.

Of course, I cannot claim that the cases, nor the tendencies they suggest, are representative of mental health services in general. The clientele and circumstances are likely to vary considerably across settings. The case material presented here does seem fairly representative of university training hospitals in terms of the patients' characteristics and the procedures of hospital staff, however, according to similar studies on the subject (Binder & McNiel, 1986; Segal, Watson, Goldfinger, & Averbuck, 1988). The cases are at least more than exceptions. They reflect the approach of those considered to be experts in their field— those who are influential in clinical decision-making and in training others to do similar work.[3]

▚ COMMITMENT OF A BATTERED WOMAN

Debra's Commitment Hearing

Debra had been brought to the psychiatric hospital the night before by her husband. He insisted that she had threatened suicide and needed to be put in the hospital. He also claimed that Debra was not taking her medications, was mistreating their 12-year-old daughter, and was doing "weird things." Even though Debra denied her husband's charges, she was admitted against her will. A commitment hearing convened 2 days later to determine if Debra could be detained in the hospital for an extended period.

At the hearing, Debra was represented by an assigned public defender who presented Debra's testimony in a clear but resigned way. The lawyer insisted in the hallway, prior to the hearing, that it was "a clear-cut" case. Debra claimed that she had been physically abused by her husband and constantly controlled by him. She also claimed that she had not been taking the full dosage of her medications because of adverse side effects. Debra had kept her daughter home from school because she thought she was ill. One of the so-called bizarre behaviors was Debra's burning of clothes, belonging to a dead relative, in the backyard. According to Debra, this was simply a convenient way to dispose of old, unwanted garments.

The husband, with help from his attorney, had testimony from the daughter and Debra's mother, as well as from a neighbor, that Debra was acting strangely and needed to be hospitalized. None of these witnesses corroborated Debra's claim of abuse. The husband pointed out that he had been counting his wife's pills to "prove" that she was not complying with her prescription.

The psychiatrist testified that he now thought the woman might be a paranoid schizophrenic, but was admittedly wavering in his diagnosis and needed more time for an evaluation. He came to this conclusion in part because Debra's description of abuse events did not "check out." The doctor also recommended hospitalization to adjust and supervise Debra's medication. Family counseling through the hospital could, as well, help any marital conflict that might exist. The psychiatrist added that the last time Debra was hospitalized, she left happily "arm-in-arm" with her husband.

Less than a month ago, Debra had been in a shelter for battered women. After repeated attempts, the battered women's advocates finally reached the public defender representing Debra at the commitment hearing.[4] They insisted that Debra had reported to them a long history of abuse—abuse from her husband and abuse from her parents when she was a child. Moreover, the battered women's advocates had had an opportunity to observe Debra during her shelter stay and found her to be mentally stable.

The battered women's advocates testified that there was more to the husband's attempt to have his wife committed. Debra was in the process of obtaining a protection from abuse (PFA) order that would prohibit her husband from seeing her for a period of time. Debra's husband took her to the hospital to head off the PFA. In addition to this testimony, the battered women's advocates offered to house and supervise Debra if she were released to them. They argued that the mental health court had the power to make an outpatient commitment of this kind and that it had an obligation to select the least restrictive option.

The battered women's advocates who witnessed the hearing felt that Debra's concerns were not heard by the all-male court and psychiatrist. The judge's brisk reply was that Debra's mother had also testified against her.

In this case, there was no clear evidence of danger to self or to others, the usual grounds for commitment, so the psychiatrist's recommendations and the weight of previous hospitalizations appeared to be the determining factor in the commitment. This is not surprising, because the decision in most commitment hearings favors the psychiatrist's recommendations, especially if the patient has been previously hospitalized. In fact, previous hospitalization is perhaps the single most influential factor assuring an extended commitment (Scheff & Culver, 1964).

Differing Interpretations

The defending lawyer aptly summarized that the case was a matter of Debra's word against her husband's. But there was more to it than that. It was also a case in which the word of psychiatry, however tentative, outweighed the arguments of battered women's advocates. This hearing represents a classic conflict of two perspectives: that prevailing in the mental health field and that of the domestic violence field. Not only did the differing perspectives shape the interpretation of the problem, they obtained competing sets of facts and recommended contrary treatments.

The mental health expert focused on the symptoms that to him suggested a serious deterioration in Debra's condition. He solicited information from the husband that sounded as if Debra might be delusional. She had allegedly been preoccupied with thoughts about dead relatives and had even been conversing with those relatives. The psychiatrist also had only a "vague" reporting of the alleged abuse from Debra and no corroborating evidence from any of the family. Debra could have easily imagined abuse when her husband tried to restrain her during her "unstable" moments, which occurred while she was not taking her prescribed medication.

The main concern of the psychiatrist is that the patient has a severe mental disorder that could become worse without hospital care. The battered women's advocates, based in the community, appear as paraprofessionals who are not trained to recognize or address severe psychopathology. As victim advocates, they tend to overidentify with victims and antagonize professional services, at least according to the private comments of the psychiatric staff at the hearing.

The battered women's advocates believed that Debra was a battered woman and that her symptoms of depression, suspicion, and even disoriented thinking could be interpreted as part of a posttraumatic stress disorder (PTSD) resulting from the abusive relationship. She was reluctant to report the details of her abuse for fear of reprisals from her husband, and did not mention being abused as a child because she feared reprisals from her mother. The husband had manipulated or intimidated the daughter to side with him, as well as obtained the collusion of Debra's abusive mother.

The greatest concern of the battered women's advocates, in this case, was the implication of the commitment decision. For one, it seemed to imply to Debra that she was to blame for the abuse. It suggested she was "crazy" and at fault for the family problems. The low self-esteem, which she may have developed from her history of abuse, was worsened in the process. The sense of isolation that victims of woman battering often experience at the hands of their abusers was also increased when Debra's voice was negated before a room full of male authorities. The commitment experience also may undermine the woman's future safety. The self-doubts engendered by the commitment could make Debra more likely to accept the abuse. A PFA will be harder to obtain, and child custody will be next to impossible.

Moreover, the commitment hearing gave further leverage to an already controlling husband. This is a man who counts his wife's medications and monitors her every move. He was able to negate his wife's attempt to assert herself using a PFA by bringing her to the hospital. He now can threaten to take Debra to the hospital if she ever steps out of line again. In the end, the perpetrator not only gets his way, he leaves thinking he is right: "It's all her fault!" And the surveillance and control continues.

▪▪ EVALUATION OF RECENTLY BATTERED WOMAN

"This appears to be a fascinating case," according to the clinician presenting her summary of the patient interview to the attending psychiatrist. Pam certainly has had an abusive and unsettled environment for much of her life. She has been abused by her husband throughout the six years of their marriage on a weekly basis. Her son has also been physically assaulted by Pam's husband and by Pam's mother. Pam was herself abused by her mother since the age of 5 and talks about recent attacks from her mother.

Although Pam admits feeling depressed about her separation from her son, who is currently residing with Children Protective Services, she insists she is not daunted by it. Besides her Bible reading, she has a job and the determination to go on. "I can't let fear and anxiety come in because I won't be a good mother."

Presentation of Victimization

Pam, a white, 35-year-old, married woman, arrived at the emergency room with her cousin. She was appropriately dressed and in a calm state. In a bold voice, she began by telling of the most recent violent incident:

> Me and my husband had an argument. His balls were hanging out and I told him to cover himself. We argued. He spat at me. My son and I got dressed and went to Burger King. He came there and we had an argument. We came back home. Two days later, my husband left. Then we were at peace. Three days later, my mother came in screaming. My brother and mother were arguing about who was to blame for my father's death. My son was scared and was under his bed.

This sort of abuse started approximately 1 year into the marriage, while the patient was 5 months pregnant. Pam discovered that her husband smoked marijuana. When she questioned him about this, an argument broke out that resulted in her husband's first attack on her.

> When I was 5 months pregnant, we were at a party. I found out my husband was on reefer. I got upset. He threw a coffee table at my stomach. Later on I got dehydrated and got pneumonia.

Pam was hospitalized for 3 days for her injuries and for the potential harm to the baby she was carrying. The husband not only continued the assaults, he began drinking heavily. At least two other hospital visits for injuries resulted. Additionally, the husband would disappear for months at a time without informing Pam of his whereabouts. Pam, consequently, had to move in with various relatives and had to rely on welfare for financial support.

Pam was also abused as a child by her mother, and was hospitalized at age 18 in response to the abuse. She denies ever striking back at her mother or provoking her mother's outbursts. Her three younger brothers were not abused. Her father was an untreated alcoholic who was apparently not physically abusive, but may have encouraged or neglected the mother's abuse of Pam.

The father's death 2 years ago seemed to revive abuse from the mother:

One night my mother came after me when I was asleep. My son made some noise and woke me up. She had a knife to my throat.

Jimmy, Pam's son, was also abused by his grandmother:

She went after him with an iron. She brainwashes him about me. Jimmy walked away one time, and the police brought him back.

The boy's father was also beating him with a belt. This prompted Pam to notify Children Protective Services. The investigation resulted in the boy's admission to Children's Hospital for protection. The husband went missing again, this time for about 4 months.

The interview then turns to the patient's ulterior motive. The clinician asks, "What do you want us to do for you?" Pam points out that she is really after an evaluation that will verify her competence before a child custody court:

I'm not mental. You can see that. I don't understand why my son left. I want my boy back. I'm not incompetent. Life can make you incompetent. If there's no roof over your head, it can make you depressed. But I go to church to take care of that.

Litigation over the custody of Pam's son was to begin shortly.

The clinician sought elaboration on the variety of abuses introduced somewhat spontaneously by the patient. "When did you first start having the problem?" asks the clinician after the initial presentation. After Pam's description of the table-throwing incident, the clinician asks about the consequences: "Were you admitted to the hospital?" Inquiries about the husband's marijuana smoking, drinking habits, and trouble with the law are made.

After a relatively thorough discussion of Pam's history of victimization, the clinician investigates a variety of psychiatric and medical symptoms. No psychiatric disorders appear, except for the patient's admitting to feeling depressed and denying that it was affecting her. There was no reported suicidality or alcohol abuse.

The patient's cousin confirms the depression in a brief exchange with the clinician. In response to the clinician's asking, "Have you noticed any changes?," Pam's cousin reports:

> She is depressed because of changes. It seems like there's no light at the end of the tunnel.

Staff Discussion

In the staff discussion, the clinician summarizes Pam's case as one of depression, but then gives detail about the abuse from the husband and mother. The clinician begins the presentation:

> The patient came in with symptoms of depression. She was feeling down about the loss of her son as he is in Children Protective Services. She says her husband and mother abused him.

After a brief statement about Pam's dating relationship with her husband, the clinician mentions the husband's initial assault:

> Five months after they were married, she found out he smoked pot. He threw a chair at her. He started drinking and abusing her.

The clinician closes her summary with reference to fights over the father's death and acknowledgment that "there seems to be a lot of fights with the mother." She then notes the custody issue: "The father walked out and is now trying to get custody."

The psychiatrist then asks the clinician several questions about Pam: "Where is the son?," and "Why is the patient here?" He seeks an elaboration of the psychiatric symptoms: "What are the symptoms? How long has this been going on? What is the patient's past psychiatric history? Does she take drugs or alcohol now? Has she been treated recently? What about medically?"

The psychiatrist also inquires about the patient's residence, financial support, and if the patient abused others. These questions are apparently to determine if there are any grounds for an involuntary commitment. In the course of the psychiatrist-clinician exchange, the clinician notes that the patient was "evasive" and "tearful" at times and some of her dates "varied."

Psychiatrist-Patient Interview

The psychiatrist's interview with the patient turns from the abuse to the depression and ends with an organic concern. The psychiatrist begins his interview with reference to the custody battle. The patient tangentially mentions yet another incident of abuse: her mother's chasing Pam's son Jimmy with a broom. The psychiatrist's only response is to ask, "Why are you telling me this?" To which the patient responds, "So you know that my husband put mental anguish on my kid."

After a few exchanges to clarify the status of the boy, the psychiatrist inquires, "What is the reason you came here?" The patient's pursuit of a support evaluation for the custody case emerges even more emphatically (PT = patient; PS = psychiatrist):

> *PT:* I need an evaluation done because my husband says I'm unstable. I get no peace and no love or understanding from my husband. This is reflected on my son. I need an evaluation to prove I'm not cracking up.
>
> *PS:* Do you think you are?
>
> *PT:* I'm depressed but that's normal for this situation I'm in.
>
> *PS:* How has this affected your thinking?
>
> *PT:* Since I've been going to church I've been better. I was a basket case before. I was scared to go to work. I was scared of men.

The patient's struggle with depressive symptoms continues to become evident as the psychiatrist asks more questions about what she does during the day and about the help she is getting with her feelings. Pam, in the process, notes that she needs to get things straightened out about her dead father.

The psychiatrist then makes a fairly lengthy check for other symptomology. Somewhat routinely he asks the patient if she has ever received a blow to her head. The question may have been in response to some of the gaps or contradictions in details—what the clinician referred to as "vagueness."

I was knocked unconscious. My mother hit me in the head with a baseball bat.

The psychiatrist's follow-up reveals that the patient received stitches, had headaches, and was tested in response to the injury.

With this, the psychiatrist ends the interview and informs Pam that she needs to be admitted to the hospital:

PS: You seem to have problems with your thoughts and remembering. Your problems need much further evaluation. . . . There also appears to be a possible need for treatment. Neurological exams and more psychiatric exams could be done faster and more comprehensively if you were in the hospital.

PT: I have a job I have to go to. I'm not coming in.

The psychiatrist comments that he "understands" and will arrange for an outpatient evaluation.

In the subsequent exchange with the clinician, the psychiatrist notes he is deferring the diagnosis until further testing:

It is a puzzling case. There may be organic factors. I don't think she is depressed. We will refer her to a primary medical center.

Case Analysis

What began as a "fascinating case" of long-term abuse ended as a "puzzling" one of possible psychiatric or organic problems. The concern over abuse was replaced with concern for brain damage. In the process, victimization was removed as a problem. Nearly one half of the initial clinician-patient interview was devoted to the extensive abuse experienced by the patient and her son. The clinician reported the specific tactic and circumstance of the initial incident of abuse in her summary of the case, but did not mention the hospitalization that resulted. The clinician acknowledged the other incidents by simply saying that the husband continued "abusing" Pam. There is no reference at this point to Pam's abuse as a child, which involved a damaging blow to the head as well as psychiatric hospitalization as a youth. The records note the patient's "marked disorganized thought process" as a central concern, and rate the staff's confidence in the obtained information as "minimal."

The psychiatric staff might argue that Pam is suffering from a repressed depression and has a preoccupation with gaining a positive evaluation for the court. Pam might in fact be considered manipulative or deceptive. She's out to make herself look good and her husband look bad for the custody case. She consistently denies any wrong doing—no present alcohol abuse, no child neglect or abuse, no retaliation toward her abusers. Her new job, church going, and care for her son are accentuated. Pam injects and returns to abusive incidents, possibly to convince the staff of her husband's and mother's incompetence.

The psychiatric staff might argue that they adequately responded to the victimization. The clinician hears out the accounts of abuse and follows them with questions about the effect and possibility of other incidents. The interaction around the victimization, in fact, exceeds that of other woman battering cases. The victimization is also cited in the clinician presentation, as well as being detailed in the written report. The fact that the patient is separated from the husband without further abusive incidents appears to be a sign of relative safety; the patient has previously reported the husband to Children Protective Services. There seems little else to be done regarding the victimization.

Moreover, the psychiatrist genuinely appears to want to help the patient. He more than once asks why the patient is telling him something and why she is there. His questions attempt to grasp the underlying process of her troubled thought and to expose the dysfunction it is causing. He introduces his final comments with "Our concern is how to help you."

The psychiatrist also concedes to the patient's refusal to enter the hospital. The psychiatrist diplomatically avoids jumping to conclusions or being unwittingly manipulated. In fact, the psychiatrist gives her what she wants, an opportunity to gain a thorough evaluation. If there are neurological problems, the patient will, of course, be better served to have them directly medically treated.

Battered women's advocates would question the psychiatric response on several counts. The psychiatric staff disregarded the battered woman's symptoms, which approximate a PTSD. Pam's acting depressed, partially immobilized, and caught in denial and repression are typical symptoms of PTSD. Rather than unrelated to the victimization or a reflection of stress, these symptoms may be the consequences of the battering. What needs to be addressed are the circumstances of her victimization.

Rather than several violent incidents, the patient suggests a constellation of controlling behaviors that have contained and suppressed her. She reports her husband's periodic desertions, his failure to offer financial support, and his control of her thoughts. None of these different aspects of abuse that so often accompany battering are explored, nor are they associated together as part of a pattern. Moreover, the patient at three different times says that she is scared of the husband's possible retaliation: "I'm afraid he'll do bad things again." Custody cases are typically a time for further threats and violence, because the woman has to oppose the battering husband publicly.

From this point of view, Pam's visit to the psychiatric hospital was a brave and progressive one. The patient's initial minimizing of her depression may have been a healthy assertion, a sign of her strength and will to get her son back and restart her life. Pam had obtained a job, reported her husband to Children Protective Services, and separated from her husband. She was reaching out for support and protection in the final showdown with her batterer. What she received, however well-intended, was an affirmation of her deficiencies. There was no advocacy, safety precautions, or acknowledgment of her dangerous situation except the psychiatrist's acknowledgment that Pam was "under a lot of stress."

■■ EVALUATION OF A WOMAN
WITH MULTIPLE PROBLEMS

"She's really faking it" is the psychiatrist's appraisal of Judy's semiconscious behavior throughout the interview. The 25-year-old black woman is brought into the emergency room slouched in a wheel chair, shabbily dressed and without shoes, and apparently in a deep sleep. It is the patient's third overdose using alcohol and Valium.

The clinician reading the patient's records comments to the psychiatrist that the patient lives with her boyfriend "who beats her regularly," has hepatitis and an ulcer, and has failed to keep outpatient appointments. The records also note a recent onset of excessive alcohol use and a diagnosis of borderline personality disorder.

To each condition, the clinician or psychiatrist makes a sarcastic remark, such as, "Regular beatings? Yeah, Tuesdays, Thursdays, and Saturdays only," and "What's the diagnosis? A 'desperate' disorder." The sarcasm throughout the interview appears, in part, as a means of coping with the unresponsiveness of a semiconscious patient and with the chaos in the emergency room during the midnight hour. The clinician is interrupted several times by phone calls, and the psychiatrist is trying to find hospital beds for other patients in need of admission.

The psychiatrist's frustration is particularly apparent in his comments to our research observer (PS = psychiatrist; OB = observer; PT = patient; CL = clinician):

> **PS:** You know, I'm getting really sick of these people here. Coming in at all times of the night with stupid shit. I want to be upstairs getting some sleep . . .
>
> **OB:** I get the impression that you think this OD was just manipulation.
>
> **PS:** Only two Valium! And she (the patient) has a history of this. I mean, what she mixed could hurt a person, but I don't think she knew that. It's really a bad attitude, I know.

Presentation of Victimization

After some jostling from the clinician and security officer, Judy wakes up enough to be questioned. After repeating the opening question three times, "Can you tell me what happened tonight?" the patient finally responds to the clinician:

> **PT:** I don't know why I took them (the pills). I'm just tired of fighting with my boyfriend.

The clinician then persistently presses the patient about the circumstances of the fight.

CL: From what I read (in the patient's records), it seems to have been a problem for awhile. . . . How long have you been seeing this guy?

PT: For about a year.

CL: So you were fighting with him today?

PT: Uh huh.

DC: And what happened?

PT: (no response)

CL: Judy, what were you arguing about?

PT: (grunt)

CL: The quicker we talk, the quicker we can get you upstairs so you can get some sleep.

PT: Yes, I'm tired. I'm just tired.

CL: I know. But I need to know what's going on. So what were you two arguing about today?

PT: I don't remember exactly. I don't remember.

CL: Did he leave?

PT: He hit me in the jaw.

CL: He hit you in the jaw. And then?

PT: (no response)

CL: What happened then?

PT: I called my sister and she . . . called the paramedics.

CL: So you took the pills after he hit you?

PT: Uh huh.

After questioning the patient about the kind of pills, her alcohol consumption, her physical health, and her medications, the clinician returns to the incident of victimization.

CL: Have you been having problems with your boyfriend?

PT: Just today.

CL: I see that at one point you were in school . . .

The clinician asks several more questions about the patient's living situation, receiving shorter and shorter responses, and he then returns to the apparent contradiction about the duration of Judy's victimization.

CL: And you and your boyfriend had no problems before
        yesterday?

PT: Uh huh.

Staff Discussion

The clinician's presentation is merely a continuation of the initial record review. The clinician and psychiatrist exchange comments about the patient's current condition, affirming her personality disorder and excessive drinking. In response to the psychiatrist's question about the amount of drinking, the clinician mentions the reported victimization:

> She's been drinking beer today, but I don't know how much. She does admit to having difficulty falling asleep. She says that she's had no problems before today—before the fight with her boyfriend . . .

> She tells me that she's tired of fighting with her boyfriend, but then she turns around and tells me that things were fine with him until today . . .

> She said that he hit her in the jaw. Oh yeah, she said the hepatitis was gone.

With an "okay," the psychiatrist is off to see the patient for himself. In a brief interchange of six questions, he asks about the apparent suicide attempt and the likelihood of another.

The clinician is then asked to call the appropriate ward and give a report on the patient. On the phone, he notes the patient's overdose, the tiredness, the boyfriend's ulcer, and the hepatitis, but he mentions nothing of the current fight or record of beating. The patient is then ushered, still drowsy, to the elevator for placement.

The written report notes, "Judy had an argument with her boyfriend that resulted in the boyfriend punching her in the jaw. The patient does not recall what the fight was about." Although listed as the only psychological stressor in the diagnostic summary, the "fights" were rated as a "mild" stressor on the report forms. The social history, collected later by a social worker, corroborates what the patient only hints in the initial emergency room interview:

The patient describes a long-standing relationship with her boy-friend, characterized by his restricting her to the house. He apparently works all day. Though she wants to leave the house, he won't let her. Apparently, this is a constant source of friction between the two of them. She denied having any other close friends at this time. In addition, she denied close contact with other family members.

Inpatient Treatment

The patient is admitted under the commitment order used to transfer her from the general hospital where she had been treated for the overdose. The main objectives are to stabilize her condition, assure compliance with medication, and deal with the "marital problems." During Judy's 7-day stay, she is described as "looking brighter" and cooperative.

The focus of the staff discussions is on the patient's several meetings with her boyfriend. The treatment summary offers this overview of the couple's counseling:

> We arranged a meeting between her boyfriend and the patient, and she was able to discuss with him how a lack of mutual understanding led to his violence towards her. She stated that during this meeting, he apologized for what he had done. She stated that she thought the reason things had gotten out of control was that her boyfriend was tired when returning from work and did not want to listen to her complaints, whereas she did not want to listen to his. Whether or not therapy will help them to listen to each other is open to question, but both were receptive to therapy at this time.

The ward clinician, perhaps anticipating the patient's discharge, prompts Judy to think about the potential for further abuse.

CL: In the future, how do you think you're going to work these things out? So you don't end up getting hit?

PT: This is the first time this has happened. Usually we talk it out . . .

CL: When you came in, you mentioned that you wanted to go to bingo and your boyfriend didn't want you to go out. My question is, did you talk about your going out and doing things on your own?

PT: Yes. He said sure. He was so tired that he didn't want me to go out.

CL: This wasn't the only time. There were other times you wanted to go out. Are you going to work on that?

PT: Yes.

The patient insists that she is ready to go home to her boyfriend after the first couple of meetings with him. After a few more days, the staff releases her to outpatient care that will include couples therapy. The patient is ready to leave the hospital because she is no longer depressed and has some potential for therapy.

The social worker concludes at the discharge meeting that Judy tends to overreact to her boyfriend and fails to take responsibility for her behavior. "That's a definite character pathology. We'll see her again." He also admits to the observer that the patient's home situation won't change much—and that might precipitate another abusive incident.

Case Analysis

Judy may well be a battered woman. The brief statement about "regular beatings" in her records is sufficient to suggest this. It is hard to imagine that her attempted overdose was merely in response to one punch to her jaw. But her insistence that there were no previous problems with her spouse undercuts any concern over her victimization.

The initial presentation of an argument that resulted in being hit is mentioned in the staff discussion. The clinician suggests a contradiction in the patient's being "tired of fighting" and "only being hit today," however. The psychiatrist's interview with the patient and the clinician makes no further mention of the victimization.

Psychiatric Staff

The informal—and incomplete—evaluation may in part be the result of the "dirty work" involved. That is, there tends to be a disregard for patients who appear undeserving and uncooperative. Judy's previous admissions for half-hearted suicide attempts and her exaggerated sleepiness leave the staff sarcastic and expedient. To his credit, the clinician does pursue the nature of the victimization, and the psychiatrist appropriately and swiftly places her. The clinicians on the ward prompt the patient to consider how to avoid further abuse; however, they arrange couples therapy to deal with the "marital problems," which may not be appropriate.

The patient's suicide attempts, alcohol abuse, and fighting with her boyfriend are linked to her personality disorder. She is overreactive and overly dependent, according to the psychiatric staff. By implication, the patient's "impulsive" behavior would be decreased through therapy that addresses her personality disorder. This sort of problem is admittedly difficult to treat, especially when the patient fails to take responsibility for his or her behavior.

Judy's history of not complying with outpatient treatment and not cooperating in the emergency room adds further doubts about her successful treatment. The ward staff do acknowledge the poor prognosis, but in a sense, they have done what they can—and are permitted to do—for the patient. They have stabilized her condition and referred her to further counseling, although they have done no planning with her to keep her safe. The patient wants to leave and returns to her spouse of her own accord.

Battered Women's Advocates

From the family violence perspective, Judy is put at great risk. Her isolation and reported violence are cues of an abusive relationship—one that she may be minimizing out of fear. Her suicide attempts may be a means of retaliating against her victimizer. It is her only means to fight back. Both the suicide attempts and the excessive alcohol use, rather than symptoms of a personality disorder, may be responses to the abusive relationship. They may be ways of easing the fear and the helplessness brought on by her boyfriend's abuse and control. Rather than being irresponsible, the patient may be accurate in identifying her boyfriend as the source of her problems.

The staff's sarcasm and suspicions in the initial interview seem to minimize the abuse. The patient is seen as a culprit in her own self-abuse. Rather than assume that Judy is "guilty" by appearances, the staff might assume that she is a "legitimate" victim until they received concrete evidence to the contrary. The patient's drowsy condition during the evaluation may itself explain her contradictory response regarding her abuse history. Regardless of the low Valium dosage, the patient is no doubt shaken by the experience. She is also still under the influence of alcohol and fatigued at that late hour of the night.

Probably the greatest concern to battered women's advocates would be the couple's meetings during Judy's inpatient stay. The patient is likely to suppress details of the abuse in response to her boyfriend's presence or coercion. Or she may be mislead by her boyfriend's false promises and apologies. In fact, Judy reports to the staff that her boyfriend profusely apologized to her during the first visit.

Moreover, it could be argued that the couple's meetings put Judy in danger; her spouse might be angered about her suicide attempt and may threaten or attack the woman. Batterers frequently interpret suicide attempts as an affront to their control, as well as a retaliation against them. A suicide attempt, furthermore, exposes the batterer to community authorities, especially if the patient explains the context of her suicide attempt.

The staff's prompting regarding the beatings might be considered inadequate and misleading. It will take much more than "talking things out" to stem further abuse, according to most battered women's advocates. Implying that the victim is also at fault tends to add to her submission and denial, rather than move her toward safety. Battered women's advocates would no doubt prefer that the woman be referred to them for additional instruction and support.

There should be some specific discussion of the options Judy has available in response to further abuse. She might even draw up a list of strategies, such as calling the police, getting a PFA order, or going to a shelter. Talking with other abused women also might help Judy understand her situation better and the options she has available. Moreover, the boyfriend might be referred or required to attend a batterer program, where his controlling and violent behavior would be more directly addressed.

■■ CONCLUSION

The case studies illustrate how the victimization of the battered women is often minimized during mental health evaluations. Although battering is likely to be reported by the clinician to the psychiatrist, the primary concern is identifying and treating the diagnosed mental disorder. Psychiatric staff might argue that the abuse is more a by-product of an underlying mental disorder that will ease as the disorder is managed.

Other complications appear to distract from the victimization. Battered women may appear to be manipulative, as in pressing for a favorable evaluation in a child custody case; or delusional, as with a chronic schizophrenic who has several previous hospitalizations. Even when the victimization is obviously genuine and unprovoked, battered women are likely to be treated for psychiatric ailments.

The potential danger to battered women appears to be ignored in the disposition. Clinicians fail to address the woman's safety with questions, precautions, information, or referrals. Outpatients are simply encouraged to return to the hospital if there are additional threats of violence, and inpatients receive couples counseling. This may in part be a reflection of the ambiguity expressed on the patients' part. Many victims resist admission; some who are admitted appear eager to return to their spouses or boyfriends after treatment.

Several underlying issues need to be taken into account. As battered women's advocates argue, many of the disorder symptoms and complications could be the manifestation of PTSD. The abuse, which is the source of the stress, needs to be addressed. Most of the women also experience stress from having to raise children without support or under threat of abuse from the children's father. Moreover, a woman's frustration over the lack of response to her pleas for help can contribute to symptoms, in which case battered women are likely to appear desperate.

Some battered women's resistance to admission may have a logical explanation. Many of the women are worried about what will happen to their children if they become an inpatient. They may have no trustworthy individuals to take care of the children while they are an inpatient, and their chances for custody might be hurt if they have a record of hospitalization. Second, battered women might appear willing to return to the victimizer because of the control he has over them through fear and manipulation of resources. Most women refer to their batterer's control of their thoughts, finances, and social relationships. Third, the threat of future violence affects most of the patients. Some women may feel that it is necessary to "face the music" and return to the batterer now, rather than later. Separation is not, in itself, a sufficient means to safety, because most of the batterers manage some contact with their partners regardless of the relationship status.

In sum, the social realities of woman battering appear to be neglected in the course of mental health evaluations—at least in those reviewed in this chapter. The case analyses suggest that differing perspectives—and the contrasting priorities of mental health clinicians—may contribute to their focus on other issues. Chapter 4, "Procedures for Assessing Woman Battering," offers a compilation of assessment tools and procedures that would enhance the response to battered women during mental health evaluations. A few basic additions to the protocol would likely increase the identification of battered women and offer more appropriate support to them.

■■ NOTES

1. Charles Lidz and Edward Mulvey of the University of Pittsburgh were coprincipal investigators of a 4-year study that focused on the violence of psychiatric patients in general. They led an extensive team of researchers and consultants in developing and implementing the study and devising the data collection and coding mechanisms. Their guidance and direction also contributed to the analysis of domestic violence cases presented here.

2. The review of additional cases of patients who were battered women confirms that the battering is often complicated by related issues. Many battered women cases also involve child abuse, sexual assault, or health problems. A few women expressed a desire to retaliate or appeared to be delusional. Some refused admission; others who appeared to want admission were referred elsewhere. In all the cases, the safety of the women remained an open and unaddressed question throughout the mental health evaluation.

3. Although these cases are taken from a hospital setting, they raise issues related to screening, assessment, treatment, and referral for mental health settings in general. The study site is a major university training hospital where mental health professionals receive instruction, serve as interns, and do their residencies. Therefore, the hospital is influential in the mental health field and, one could argue, reflects accepted practices in the field. The cases themselves may represent more severe and complicated cases than tend to appear at a community mental health center. At the same time, these cases may have appeared at a community mental health clinic if the clinic had been more convenient for the patients, and the cases could easily have been referred to a mental health clinic from the hospital for outpatient care.

4. Debra had contacted the battered women's advocates about her commitment hearing and asked them to help her. At that time, she also gave the shelter permission to release information about her shelter stay.

4

Procedures for Assessing Woman Battering

Assessment Tools

Assessment of woman battering can be a difficult and complex task given the nature of abuse, the diversity of its effects, and threats to personal safety. Procedures combining experience from battered women's programs and developments in the mental health field can significantly increase the identification of battered women and improve the assessment of their battering, however. Several instruments, tools, and guides have been developed to address the needs and circumstances of battered women more effectively.

Specific tools or guides fit with the procedures common to mental health services, especially screening, evaluation, diagnosis, treatment, and record keeping (see Dutton, 1992a; Saunders, 1992a). Therefore, they may be readily integrated into the conventional protocol or procedures of most mental health services.

Screening questions help identify women who are highly likely to have been abused or battered. An *assessment instrument* may be used to establish the extent and nature of the woman's abuse and offer an objective measure of the severity for comparisons. An *abuse history and*

65

lethality inventory serves to evaluate the kind, pattern, duration, influence, and risks of the abuse. A *safety plan* addresses some of the identified dangers and risks. A *diagnostic process* that considers symptoms in the context of the abuse and the high likelihood of posttraumatic stress disorder (PTSD) among battered women is less likely to be detrimental or inappropriate. Reporting in clinical records and/or to related agencies that avoids vagaries and details the abuse is also important. It can help focus on the abuse in treatment and provide documentation for further interventions and assistance.

This chapter recommends instruments, tools, and guides that might be used in each of these procedures to identify and assess woman battering. Preliminary research and practical experience suggest that these instruments will significantly increase the identification of battered women, increase their satisfaction with mental health services, and improve their situation and circumstances (see Dutton, 1992b; Gondolf, 1990; Saunders, 1992a).

Evaluation Procedures

The procedures of mental health services are very different than those familiar to many battered women's advocates. This is in part because the objectives and purposes of mental health services tend to differ from those of battered women's programs. So do the training, experience, and outlook of the respective staffs, as discussed in Chapter 3, "Case Studies of Mental Health Evaluations." Mental health services are also influenced by the need to establish a psychological or psychiatric diagnosis that conforms to the categories established in the *Diagnostic and Statistical Manual of Mental Disorders* (American Psychiatric Association, 1994). Customary assessment and evaluation procedures make up the process of making a diagnosis. This chapter is organized around specific steps customarily involved in the evaluation process used in mental health services. The steps are arranged in the same order as they are likely to be conducted in a mental health service. Not all the steps are necessarily conducted in all mental health services, nor are all necessarily appropriate for all cases. Most of the steps are routinely employed in some formal or informal protocol, however.

Mental health professionals generally begin their contact with potential clients by conducting an evaluation to determine the nature and extent of the client's psychological and/or psychiatric problems (Shea,

1988). They are particularly intent on establishing a diagnosis that categorizes these problems, implies certain treatments, and allows for payment reimbursements. The diagnoses, based on the *Diagnostic and Statistical Manual*, may range from major mental disorders (Axis I) such as schizophrenia and manic-depressive disorder, to personality problems (Axis II) such as dependent, borderline, or antisocial personality disorders. Clinicians may also identify situational problems such as adjustment disorder or mild depression. A diagnosis provides for identification of related social and relationship stressors (V codes) as well.

The evaluation process generally includes screening, assessment, establishing a diagnosis, treatment recommendations, and clinical reports. The first step in the evaluation is to *screen* for serious problems that require extensive and immediate response, such as suicide, alcoholism, and organic dysfunction. A few broad questions are routinely asked of clients to help identify the possibility of such serious problems. Battered women's advocates generally recommend that mental health professionals routinely screen for battering.

The second step in the evaluation is to *assess* the extent and nature of the problems identified in the screening. Structured assessment instruments are frequently used to provide some objective measure of the problem. For instance, the Addiction Severity Index (McLellan et al., 1985) is widely used in the drug and alcohol field to assess those suspected of having drug and alcohol problems. Such assessment tools have been shown to enhance the identification of problems beyond open-ended clinical observations or questioning. Some sample assessment instruments for battering and a discussion of the major issues surrounding their implementation are provided below.

Battered women's advocates recommend that an additional step be taken at this point. An *abuse history* should be developed through a series of open-ended questions that prompt an account of the patterns and effects of abuse. *Safety planning* should also be conducted using appropriate questions and inventory of possible strategies to reduce the risk of recurrent or escalating abuse. Safety planning often includes a *lethality assessment* that attempts to determine the risk of homicide or serious danger in general.

The diagnostic evaluation may be part of a broader social history, or may stand alone as a focused effort to identify relevant symptomatology. Some of the questions may attempt to rule out certain diagnoses, and others may help explore other possibilities. Most diagnoses are considered tentative at an initial evaluation or intake interview and require further observation or questioning during treatment to confirm or revise them. Advocates raise some cautions to help ensure that battered women receive the most appropriate diagnosis, and recommend that special consideration be given to the possibility of PTSD.

Finally, most mental health professionals are required to write a *clinical report* summarizing their assessment, evaluation, and treatment recommendations. Researchers have identified tendencies to avoid and information to include to document woman battering and ensure its prominence in the clinical report. Appropriate safety provisions, treatment goals, and referrals for woman battering also need to be recorded.

▪▪ SCREENING QUESTIONS

In a study of mental health intake procedures, twice the number of clients disclosed abuse in response to a structured interview about abuse than to a conventional intake interview (Saunders, Kilpatrick, & Resnick, 1989). Research on hospital emergency rooms and psychiatric evaluation centers documents that conventional screening will identify only 15 to 25% of the battered women entering these services (Gondolf, 1990; Jacobson et al., 1987; Warshaw, 1989). The systematic use of concrete indicators, however, substantially increases the identification. Specific closed-ended questions for woman battering, similar to those employed in suicide screening, need to be asked routinely, especially given the disproportionately high numbers of battered and abused women that visit mental health services (Gondolf, 1990; Jacobson & Richardson, 1987; McFarlane, Parker, Soeken, & Bullock, 1992; McLeer & Anwar, 1989).

Several screening tools for woman battering have been developed for settings as diverse as mediation courts and hospital emergency rooms (Girder, 1990; Marshall, 1992; McFarlane, et al., 1992). They tend to offer a combination of questions about different kinds of abusive behaviors highly associated with battering. Battered women frequently deny or minimize their battering out of fear, distrust, or subjection. Asking about a range of indicators, therefore, is helpful in exposing the possibility of severe abuse. A positive answer to any one question warrants follow-up and further investigation of woman abuse.

Figure 4.1 presents a set of screening and follow-up questions recommended for routine use in mental health services. The questions are derived

Screening Questions

1. Are you in any way fearful of your partner?
2. Does your partner have angry outbursts or temper tantrums?
3. Has your partner stopped you from going places or seeing people?
4. Has your partner threatened to harm you, your children, or your relatives?
5. Has your partner ever pushed, grabbed, slapped, or hit you?
6. Has your partner ever pressured you into sexual acts against your will?

Follow-Up Questions

NOTE: Each screening question with a positive response should be followed with probes for the most recent incident, duration, frequency, effect, and response to incidents.

A. When was the most recent incident?
B. How long has this been going on?
C. How often has it happened in the last 6 months?
D. How has it made you feel? How has it hurt you physically?
E. What help or assistance have you sought?
F. How do you feel about calling the police or going to court to receive assistance?

Figure 4.1. Screening and Follow-up Questions for Woman Battering

by combining several of the available screening tools and weighing them against preliminary research about screening for woman battering. The major shortcoming with this tool, and other screening tools, is that its accuracy (sensitivity and specificity) has not been scientifically measured. As medical sociology research shows, the accuracy of even sophisticated biomedical screening is very difficult to determine (Russell, 1994). The indication is, however, that the use of such a screening tool substantially increases the identification of abuse for up to 90% of the known battered women in preliminary studies (McLeer & Anwar, 1989; Warshaw, 1989).

▉▉ ASSESSMENT INSTRUMENTS

There are more than 10 published assessment instruments for woman battering that offer validated and standardized measures of the extent and nature of abuse and battering (e.g., Hudson & McIntosh, 1981; Marshall, 1992; Shepard & Campbell, 1992; Straus, 1979). These instruments use from 15 to over 50 closed-ended questions in the form of a structured inventory of abusive behaviors, and provide a scoring system for the total severity of abuse. Validity and reliability tests are offered for the instruments, but debate remains over their interpretation (see Straus, 1990). Much of the discrepancy lies in the conceptualization of abuse as discrete events defined by behavioral tactics. Many researchers of violence view abuse and battering as a process with a range of effects and meanings that most instruments do not consider (Morrison, 1988; Mulvey & Lidz, 1993). Moreover, documented discrepancies exist between men's and women's reports, and scores are generally elevated by counseling or advocacy (Arias & Beach, 1987; Edleson & Syers, 1990). Even with the shortcomings, a few of the instruments are widely used because they provide a standardized means of measurement and comparison beyond screening questions and clinical evaluations.

A woman battering instrument might be administered to women screened as battered women to gauge more specifically the nature and extent of their abuse. In some services, the self-administered instrument may substitute for the more informal screening process to expedite the intake process. The measurement of the abuse may also be helpful in alerting a woman to the severity of her situation, in developing safety plans, and in prescribing intervention and treatment. Some measurement is also important in developing a statistical overview of abuse cases for administrative and programming reports, as is often done with crime statistics in the criminal justice field.

Figure 4.2 presents the Index of Spouse Abuse (ISA) as a recommended instrument for the standardized assessment of woman battering and abuse (Hudson & McIntosh, 1981). The ISA has 30 items that are relatively easy to answer in about 5 minutes. One of its advantages is that about two thirds of the items address nonphysical abuse in the form of both instrumental (controlling) abuse and emotive (anger-based) abuse. Another advantage over other instruments is that the ISA offers weights for the severity or potential effect of each item.[1] A composite scoring therefore offers a measure of overall severity that includes the nonphysical abuse. Moreover, the ISA has two subscales that may be scored separately: a subscale for nonphysical abuse that includes the items numbered next to NP at the bottom of the index, and a subscale

This questionnaire is designed to measure the degree of abuse you have experienced in your relationship with your partner. It is not a test, so there are no right or wrong answers. Answer each item as carefully and accurately as you can by placing a number beside each one as follows:

1 = Never; 2 = Rarely; 3 = Occasionally; 4 = Frequently; 5 = Very frequently

_____ 1. My partner belittles me. (1)
_____ 2. My partner demands obedience to his whims. (17)
_____ 3. My partner becomes surly and angry if I tell him he is drinking too much. (15)
_____ 4. My partner makes me perform sex acts which I do not enjoy or like. (50)
_____ 5. My partner becomes very upset if dinner, housework, or laundry is not done when he thinks it should be. (4)
_____ 6. My partner is jealous and suspicious of my friends. (8)
_____ 7. My partner punches me with his fists. (75)
_____ 8. My partner tells me I am ugly and unattractive. (26)
_____ 9. My partner tells me I really couldn't manage or take care of myself without him. (8)
_____ 10. My partner acts like I am his personal servant. (20)
_____ 11. My partner insults or shames me in front of others. (41)
_____ 12. My partner becomes very angry if I disagree with his point of view. (15)
_____ 13. My partner threatens me with a weapon. (82)
_____ 14. My partner is stingy in giving me enough money to run our home. (12)
_____ 15. My partner belittles me intellectually. (20)
_____ 16. My partner demands that I stay home to take care of the children. (14)
_____ 17. My partner beats me so badly that I must seek medical help. (98)
_____ 18. My partner feels that I should not work or go to school. (21)
_____ 19. My partner is not a kind person. (13)
_____ 20. My partner does not want me to socialize with my female friends. (18)
_____ 21. My partner demands sex whether I want it or not. (52)
_____ 22. My partner screams and yells at me. (38)
_____ 23. My partner slaps me around my face and head. (80)
_____ 24. My partner becomes abusive when he drinks. (65)
_____ 25. My partner orders me around. (29)
_____ 26. My partner has no respect for my feelings. (39)
_____ 27. My partner acts like a bully towards me. (44)
_____ 28. My partner frightens me. (55)
_____ 29. My partner treats me like a dunce. (29)
_____ 30. My partner acts like he would like to kill me. (80)
P = 3, 4, 7, 13, 17, 2-24, 27, 28, 30; NP = 1, 2, 5, 6, 8-12, 14-16, 18-21, 25, 26, 29

Figure 4.2. Index of Spouse Abuse

SOURCE: Hudson & McIntosh (1981). The assessment of spouse abuse: Two quantifiable dimensions. *Journal of Marriage and the Family, 43,* 873-884. Copyrighted (1981) by the National Council on Family Relations, 3989 Central Ave. NE, Suite 550, Minneapolis, MN.

for physical abuse indicated by the items next to P. (See the note for further information on scoring.)

The Conflict Tactic Scale (Straus, 1979) is probably the most widely used assessment instrument, and is therefore recommended by some researchers (see Saunders, 1992a). Debate over its emphasis on physical tactics, omission of effect and severity, and questioned scoring system makes an alternative advisable, however. Some of the other available instruments, such as the Maltreatment of Women Scale (Tolman, 1989), are more comprehensive, but very long (approximately 50 questions) and not sufficiently validated. Other measures for wife-beating beliefs, control, and proprietariness may prove to be better indicators for woman battering than the behaviorist measures currently in use, but they need further development and validation before they can be routinely employed. Moreover, some instruments are being promoted that are based on debatable assumptions about woman battering and questionable validation.

None of the instruments is a substitute for an in-depth abuse history conducted face-to-face with open-ended questioning and discussion, but an assessment instrument might be used as a basis for the abuse history and to facilitate a history interview. The interviewer can ask the woman to describe the circumstances, effect, and response to each of the items answered affirmatively. The overall scores may also provide a basis for discussion about the severity of the abuse and its consequences.

■■ ABUSE HISTORY

Contributions

A study of women in a psychiatric outpatient clinic found that nearly 70% of the women had experienced major physical or sexual assaults, but that nearly three fourths of those patients had never before disclosed the experience of abuse to a clinician despite in-depth social history interviews (Jacobson, 1989). Psychologists and psychiatrists working with battered women strongly recommend that a separate abuse history be conducted with identified battered women to obtain this important information (Browne, 1993; Dutton, 1992b; Warshaw, 1993). The abuse history is essential to discern the dynamics, types, pattern, and effect of abuse. Screening and assessment instruments do not by themselves determine the effect and consequence of abuse and battering.

An abuse history serves several specific functions. It provides a fuller picture of the woman's experience with abuse that is needed for determining the trauma she has experienced. Identifying this trauma is important for diagnosis and treatment recommendations. The abuse history helps put symptomatology in a broader context, which may alter the interpretation of those symptoms, as discussed below. Also, an abuse history provides information needed to develop a safety plan for the woman.

The abuse history has a more immediate role for the battered woman. It helps validate her experience and alert her to the seriousness of her situation (Dutton, 1992b; Warshaw, 1993). The abuse history can help a woman more accurately assess her own situation and reinforce the need for her to make necessary decisions about her well-being. It helps counter the tendency to cope with abuse by denying or minimizing it, accepting the rationalizations of one's abuser, or listening to other caretakers who have dismissed or neglected the abuse.

Realizing the dynamics of one's abuse often facilitates an *attributional shift* in which a battered woman begins to see her batterer as responsible for the battering, rather than blaming herself for the man's abusive behavior. This shift is usually associated with a willingness to take action to protect oneself more substantially than simply trying to fix the situation (Gondolf & Fisher, 1988; Holtzworth-Munroe, 1988). Therefore, battered women often insist that one of the most important steps in their healing process is to have their abuse experience validated and acknowledged.

Tools

Figure 4.3 presents an inventory of types and tactics of abuse that is often used to begin an abuse history. The Index of Spouse Abuse includes several of these tactics, but does not categorize or name them as this inventory does. The inventory is drawn from the "power and control wheel," which is a widely used pictorial illustration of the different forms of abuse (see Pence & Paymar, 1993). Some clinicians may prefer to use this wheel as a visual aide in conducting the abuse history. Others might simply follow the inventory in Figure 4.3 by first naming each category and then asking if the woman has experienced each of the items in that

Isolation

- Keeping the victim from going to a job, school, church, or from seeing family and friends
- Taking away the victim's ID cards or driver's license
- Following the victim around
- Opening the woman's mail
- Monitoring phone calls or removing telephone

Financial Control

- Denying access to money
- Forcing the woman to beg and plead for money
- Lying about money or hiding it
- Preventing the victim from working
- Stealing the victim's money
- Not providing sufficient money for expenditures
- Ruining or preventing the woman from getting credit
- Threatening to jeopardize her receipt of AFDC

Intimidation

- Frightening the woman by certain gestures and looks
- Smashing or throwing things
- Destroying the woman's possessions
- Hurting or killing pets
- Playing with weapons to scare the woman
- Threatening to kill the woman, children, or himself
- Threatening to have the woman deported, if immigrant or refugee status

Figure 4.3. Types and Tactics of Woman Abuse
SOURCE: Pence & Paymar (1993).

category. An introduction for each category might include, "Many women experience abuse in the form of 'financial control' (category of abuse), in which their partners try to control or subject them by withholding or misusing money (description of tactics)."

Figure 4.4 presents a set of questions to develop a more in-depth history of abuse and battering. The object of the questions is first to lead the woman through a description of the pattern of her abuse: the when and where, how and why, and highs and lows. The second objective is

Emotional Abuse

- Putting the woman down
- Calling the woman names
- Humiliating the woman in front of family and friends
- Making the woman feel stupid
- Blaming the woman for what he did wrong

Sexual Abuse

- Ridiculing the woman's sexual performance or response
- Pressuring the woman to do sex acts that make her uncomfortable
- Threatening to sexually molest the children
- Pressuring the woman to copy pornographic magazines
- Pressuring the woman to watch pornographic videos
- Raping or threatening to rape

Physical Abuse

- Pushing, shoving, grabbing, arm twisting
- Slapping, punching, choking, burning, beating up
- Use of objects or weapons against the woman

Figure 4.3. *Continued*

to have the woman describe the effect of the abuse: how it has affected her emotionally, behaviorally, and spiritually. The clinician might especially notice dangers, risks, cycles, and escalation in the abuse and the symptoms associated with PTSD.

Some clinicians may want to turn the items listed in Figure 4.4 into a semistructured interview; others might want to use them as probes in an unstructured interview, encouraging the woman to tell her story (see Dutton, 1992b). A few structured instruments have been used to assess the traumatic effect of abuse more systematically, although they have not been substantially tested on battered women. They include the Impact of Event Scale (Horwitz, Wilner, & Alvarez, 1979) and the MMPI-2 (PTSD subscale; Keane, Malloy, & Fairbank, 1984).

Verification

One of the barriers to evaluations of battered women in the past has been that their stories of abuse are occasionally disbelieved. There are

Describe the Pattern of Abuse

- The first time your partner abused or frightened you, and when this happened
- The worst incident or type of abuse, and when this happened
- The most frightening or scary times or incidents, and when these happened
- The frequency of emotional, physical, and sexual abuse over the entire relationship, last year, and last month
- The circumstances of severe, brutal, or dangerous abuse
- Incidence of abuse occurring around pregnancy, separations, unemployment, or substance abuse
- Your partner's excessive discipline or abuse of children
- Your partner's assault or violence toward others and his breaking the law or being arrested

Describe the Effect of Abuse

- Changes in yourself over the course of the relationship
- Changes in relationship between you and your children
- Not going certain places or seeing certain people
- Avoidance of certain subjects or situations with partner
- Your calling the police, going to court, running away, contacting a shelter, or telling a friend or relative about abuse
- Fears you have for your or your children's safety
- Your view of life in general, your hopes for a better situation, your faith in a spiritual or higher power
- Fears of going crazy, being paralyzed with fear, or wanting to lash out
- Symptoms of depression, suicide, anxiety, substance abuse, physical injury, and trauma

Figure 4.4. Abuse History Questions
SOURCE: Adapted from Schechter (1994).

documented cases of battered women being involuntarily committed to psychiatric hospitals, despite claims that their partners were abusing and coercing them (Gondolf, 1990; Warshaw, 1993). Claims of abuse or battering may have been categorized as delusion or paranoia. Clinicians may also doubt a woman's reports because she has not disclosed the information in previous mental health visits or to friends or relatives. There are some practical reasons for these tendencies. Battered women may be reluctant to disclose their abuse because they are accustomed to being disbelieved, blamed, or threatened. Their abusers are also likely to minimize, deny, or rationalize what has happened. In some cases, they manipulate family members, police, and social service providers to be against the battered woman and counter her story. In the process, the abuser appears very rational and convincing, whereas the fearful and exasperated woman is likely to appear nervous and evasive—and therefore less credible.

If a clinician has doubts about a woman's story, he or she might ask about other sources of documentation: police, court, or hospital records. Neighbors or friends might have overheard incidents of abuse, or the woman might be able to show some visible injury. Moreover, the clinician might inquire about childhood sexual molestation or physical abuse. What appears as a "delusion" or paranoia may be related to actual past experiences.

▉ SAFETY PLANNING

The safety of battered women is one of the primary concerns of battered women's advocates and program staff. The abuse is likely to escalate over time and particularly intensify when battered women seek help or attempt separation or divorce (Walker, 1984; Wilson & Daly, 1993). In fact, battered women are more than twice as likely to be killed when they are attempting to separate from their abuser (Wilson & Daly, 1993). Children are also frequently harmed, threatened, or held hostage as a way to retaliate against a battered woman who is seeking help. A batterer may view a woman's visiting a mental health service as a threat. He may think that the woman is going to report him to authorities for punishment or to get assistance to leave him.

Battered women's programs routinely do safety plans and lethality assessments to help them make appropriate referrals and take protective action and to assist the woman in compiling information needed to make decisions and plans for herself and her children (see Hart & Stuehling, 1992). There is no formal research established on the effectiveness of these plans, but they do appear to heed the recommendations of related studies. Research on formerly battered women indicates that women were the safest who employed a diversity of strategies to avoid or interrupt the abuse (Bowker, 1993; Sullivan, Basta, Cheribeth, & Davidson,

1992). The safety plans help battered women raise and consider such strategies.

Figure 4.5 presents a lethality checklist that might accompany an abuse history (Hart, 1992). The purpose of the lethality checklist is to alert the woman and staff to behaviors associated with increased risk of injury and homicide. This checklist is derived from a review of battered women's homicides and preliminary research on lethality assessment (Campbell, 1986). Some debate remains over the utility of such an assessment because homicide is so difficult to predict: Assessment checklists grossly overpredict homicide and may in some cases mislead battered women (see Gondolf & Hart, 1994; Sherman, Schmidt, Rogan, & DeRiso, 1991). The items on the checklist are highly associated with more severe abuse, however, and therefore can further expose the severity of current abuse, if not predict lethality (Gondolf, 1988a; Saunders, 1994). Figure 4.5 can be used as an inventory by asking the woman if her abuser has exhibited each behavior. The interviewer might use the descriptions in parentheses as probes, and follow up affirmative answers with requests to "describe," "explain," or "elaborate."

Figure 4.6 offers an adaptation and consolidation of the prevailing safety planning guides used by many battered women's programs (Hart & Stuehling, 1992). It outlines precautions and steps to take to identify potentially abusive situations and precautions to avoid or escape battering. It also helps educate women about possible sources of help, support, and protection. The clinician should ask the woman each question, probing for clarification and elaboration where necessary. The responses should be written down to formulate a plan of action that is confirmed with the woman. The plan should be kept on file and reviewed regularly with the woman to make revisions and to remind the woman of the plan. Ideally, this planning process will promote a pattern of thinking that will lead the battered woman toward protective actions.

Figure 4.7 provides a list of practical suggestions that have been used by other battered women to protect themselves. The suggestions focus on efforts to separate from the batterer when retaliation or pursuit is especially likely. This list might be reviewed and explained to a woman and turned into a checklist to note steps she has taken and might consider taking in the future. Some advocates caution against giving the safety plans or safety suggestions to a woman to take with her. Her abuser may become angry and abusive if he finds them. It is not uncommon for an

- Threats of homicide or suicide ("I'm going to get you," "You'll pay for this," "I'll kill myself if you leave.")
- Fantasies of homicide or suicide (ideas, thoughts, or plans about killing—the more detailed the more dangerous)
- Weapon possession, use, and threats (ready access to and familiarity with guns, knives, arson, etc.)
- "Ownership" of the battered woman ("You belong to me and will never belong to another!")
- Centrality of woman (idolizing the battered woman and depending heavily on her to sustain his life)
- Separation violence and threats (great despair or rage when the battered woman leaves or considers leaving)
- Attempted pursuit, stalking, hostage taking (of battered woman, children, or other relatives)
- Escalation of personal risk (behavior that disregards legal or social consequences)
- Extreme depression and alcohol or drug binges (noticeable erratic changes in mood or behavior)

Figure 4.5. Lethality Checklist for Woman Battering
SOURCE: Hart (1992).

abuser to go through a woman's things or pressure her to give him what she has received from a visit to a mental health service or other support program.

DIAGNOSIS

Issues

The most controversial area of mental health services with battered women is diagnosis. As discussed in Part I of this book, many battered women's advocates believe that any psychiatric diagnosis misrepresents the social circumstances of battering and is detrimental to battered women (see Schechter, 1994; Worell & Remer, 1992). A psychiatric diagnosis implies that a battered woman's problems are associated primarily with some internal disorder or pathology, rather than a response to

Notice Cues of Possible Violence
- What situations or conflicts tend to lead to abuse?
- When and where do most abusive incidents occur?
- What expressions, comments, or gestures come before abusive incidents?

Know a Quick Escape Route
- How would you quickly exit your house to avoid a violent incident?
- What doors, windows, elevators, stairwells or fire escapes would you use?
- Where could you leave your car keys and purse to leave quickly?
- Where will you go to stay or get help (friends, relatives, women's shelter)?

Prepare Others to Call the Police
- What neighbors or friends can you tell to call the police if they hear suspicious noises coming from your house?
- What do you need to teach your children so they could telephone the police if there is an incident?
- What code word could you use to alert children and friends to call for help?
- What will you tell the police if they do come to your house?

Know Sources of Help and Support
- What are the women's shelter or domestic violence hotline numbers in your area?
- What are the names of battered women's advocates and how can you reach them?
- What is the best way to call the police and what would you tell them if you called?
- What are the steps for securing a protection order in your area?
- Where is the nearest hospital emergency room and what is the quickest way to get there?

Figure 4.6. Safety Plan Guide
SOURCE: Adapted from Hart & Stuehling (1992).

external abuse and battering. Treatments are too often prescribed on the basis of the disorders and neglect the abuse and the trauma it causes (Gondolf, 1990; Herman, 1992; Janoff-Bulman, 1992). Moreover, the stigma associated with many diagnoses leaves women trapped in the mental health system and may be used against them in divorce and custody litigation. A battered woman, as a result, may end up feeling invalidated and demeaned and may continue to blame herself for the abuse.

Diagnoses that account for abuse and battering may have some merit (Browne, 1993; Dutton, 1992a; Saunders, 1992a). An appropriate diagnosis may entitle a woman to needed and deserved psychological services. Certain diagnoses are needed for hospital admission or insurance reimbursement. In many cases, insurance reimbursement for treatment is not available without a diagnosis. Moreover, a battered woman is more likely to receive treatment for the trauma and effects of abuse and battering if she has a specific diagnosis related to it. Some battered women have chronic mental problems that need extensive psychiatric care that comes only with a diagnosis.

One related shortcoming is that women with low incomes are more likely to receive diagnoses of chronic mental disorders and end up with inadequate treatment. Those with the ability to pay are more likely to be accepted at private or training mental health facilities. These facilities are more attentive to alternative diagnoses and treatments that consider abuse and battering. The majority of battered women in battered women's programs are in poverty, often as a result of separation from their abusive partner, and unable to afford the better mental health services.

Battered women have been evaluated with a variety of mental disorders: most frequently, major depression, paranoid schizophrenia, dependent personality disorder, and borderline personality disorder (Gleason, 1993; Gondolf, 1990; Herman, 1992). As summarized in Figure 4.8, the symptoms of these disorders assume a different meaning in the context of abuse. For instance, alcohol and drug abuse may be a means of sedating the pain and distress many battered women experience, or may be the result of pressure from one's abusive partner to use alcohol or drugs with him.

Many apparent symptoms may be expected reactions and adaptations to the trauma of abuse (see Campbell, 1993; Dutton, 1992a; Kemp et al., 1991). They may be very logical or necessary means of coping with the abuse. Therefore, dissuading or extinguishing some "symptoms" may endanger women by taking away needed coping and protective strategies. Failure to address the abuse and the trauma associated with it may result, moreover, in ineffective and even counterproductive treatment (Dutton, 1992b; Herman, 1992; Janoff-Bulman, 1992).

Avoiding Your Partner
(after a protection order or separation)

- Use an answering machine or a phone signal to screen your phone calls at home.
- Have someone at work help screen your phone calls.
- Plan a route leaving work to avoid accidental contact with your partner.
- Plan an escape route if you encounter your partner at work, on the street, in a shopping place.
- Use different grocery stores, malls, and banks at different hours to avoid contact with your partner.

Safety With Protection Orders

- Keep a copy of your protection order on or near you.
- Change locks, keep windows locked, install an alarm, and get steel doors (if possible).
- Give copies of the order to police departments in communities where you work, where relatives live, and where you live.
- Check with the court registry of protection orders to be sure your order is in the registry.
- File your protection order in other counties that you plan to visit.
- Inform your employer, minister, and closest friend that you have an order of protection.
- Contact the local courthouse if you lose your order or your partner destroys it.
- Call the police, attorney, shelter advocate, and/or court if your partner violates the order.
- File a complaint with the police department if the police do not help in a violation.
- File a criminal complaint with the district judge if your partner violates the order.
- Call a local battered women's program or women's shelter if you need help registering your order, notifying police departments, or filing complaints.

Figure 4.7. Additional Safety Suggestions

Common Diagnoses

The most common disorder noticed in battered women is depression (Campbell, 1995; Campbell, Sullivan, & Davidson, 1995). There is no

Items for Leaving

- Extra set of keys
- Spare cash
- Change for phone calls (avoid using credit cards)
- Separate savings account
- Extra clothes and bedding
- Identification cards, driver's license, and car registration
- Credit cards in your name only
- Checkbook and bank card (in your name only)
- Personal pictures and special items
- Jewelry and other valuables
- Children's favorite toys and blankets
- Important documents (birth certificates, social security cards, school and vaccination records, welfare identification, work permits, green card, passports, divorce papers, medical records, lease, deed, mortgage payment, bank books, insurance papers)

Figure 4.7. *Continued*

SOURCE: Adapted from Hart & Stuehling (1992).

NOTE: As many of these items as possible should be stored at a friend's house or in a prepacked suitcase so that they can be grabbed quickly.

doubt that many battered women feel disappointed, discouraged, saddened, and even suicidal as a result of the battering. The trauma of being battered itself may contribute to a sense of loss and dejection. The battering may undo one's ideals about relationships, love, and home. Advocates have noted that many women go through a grieving process in response to a "death" of their relationship caused by the battering (Carmen, 1995; Turner & Shapiro, 1986). The appearance of depression may also be a response to the verbal and psychological abuse that tend to accompany battering (Cascardi & O'Leary, 1992). Women who are continually put down, degraded, ridiculed, and yelled at may incorporate a negative view of themselves and the world around them.

Batterers also frequently isolate their victims by limiting their contacts with family and friends, keeping them from going out alone, and not allowing them to have a job or attend school. The lack of social

- Isolated incidents of abuse appear as a pattern of control and degradation
- Self-blame appears as result of invalidation and sense of personal responsibility
- Denial, fear, and depression reappear as acute reactions to trauma
- Symptomatology is redefined as coping strategies to deal with abuse
- Mental disorders appear as having an external social origin in abuse and battering
- Substance abuse appears as means to self-medicate pain of victimization and trauma, or from pressure by abusive partner
- Learned helplessness appears more the result of entrapment and lack of options
- "Hysteria" and passivity appear as intrusive and avoidance phases of PTSD

Figure 4.8. Redefining Symptoms in Context of Woman Battering

support in itself contributes to a sense of loneliness, disconnection, and ultimately depression. Furthermore, many battered women become depressed over the lack of—ineffectiveness of—services, police response, and help from friends. Many women feel, as a result, that nothing can be done to stop the abuse. They feel trapped, deserted, and helpless (Campbell et al., 1995).

In sum, depressive disorders are very likely to be a response to the circumstances of woman battering, and therefore need to be put in the context of battering. Addressing the circumstances of the battering may in some cases alleviate the depressive symptoms that antidepressants may otherwise only temporarily relieve. Moreover, addressing the depression alone with antidepressants may relieve symptoms that signal distress and danger in a relationship and contribute to a woman's tolerating an abusive relationship.

The next most prevalent major disorder applied to battered women is a dissociative disorder (Koss et al., 1994). The disorder tends to be associated with women who have an extended history of abuse and trauma, including incidents of child abuse and rape. Advocates in the trauma field argue that dissociative symptoms, such as confusion about one's identity or inability to recall important personal information, may be formed as coping strategies. They help an individual protect herself from the influence of traumatic events and the pain experienced in recalling them (Chu & Dill, 1990). Panic attacks, anxiety disorders, and affective disorders may be similarly related to an abusive relationship.

Battered women have frequently been diagnosed as having a wide range of personality disorders, as well (Gondolf, 1990; Stark & Flitcraft, 1988). They tend to be diagnosed as having a hysterical, borderline, dependent, or passive-aggressive disorder, but no personality or charac-terological commonalties have been established for battered women (Walker & Browne, 1985). The long-standing concern among advocates is that these diagnoses are often confused with a woman's efforts to cope with the abuse situation. A battered woman may appear manipulative or antisocial as a means of fighting back or asserting some control with an otherwise dominating partner. Symptoms related to a dependent personality may reflect a woman's inability to make decisions in a very controlling relationship in which her partner treats her like an infant, degrades her for her input, and punishes her for her initiatives. Address-ing these symptoms without considering the dynamics of the battering may, in some cases, curb a woman's means of coping and protecting herself (see Brown, 1992).

A personality disorder, similar to major psychiatric disorders, may also be related to a woman's trauma history. According to recent research on the topic, the vast majority of women diagnosed with personality disorders were abused during childhood or adolescence (Herman, 1992). Symptoms associated with personality disorders may also be related to antidepressant medication or other medicine battered women are taking to deal with their emotional and physical problems related to abuse and battering (Mahoney, 1991). The medications may, for instance, be causing passive behavior in a woman who may otherwise be more expressive, active, and whole.

The implication is that the common diagnoses of battered women should be made with some caution, and only after circumstantial expla-nations of the symptoms and the likelihood of PTSD are ruled out. As discussed below, PTSD is a disorder that accounts for a variety of symptoms often confused with other disorders. It also implies that the symptoms are a response to abuse or battering. If symptoms do appear to supersede a woman's abuse history and are best indicated by a major disorder (Axis I) or personality disorder (Axis II), a couple of steps might be taken to ensure attention to the battering. Appropriate V codes should be used to identify the related problem of abuse (V61.1 to indicate "physical abuse of an adult" and an additional code 995.81 to indicate the patient is the victim). Woman battering can additionally be identified on the Axis IV used for reporting psychosocial and environmental problems.

PTSD

At least one established diagnostic category alleviates most of the prevalent concerns associated with the diagnoses that battered women commonly receive. A growing number of mental health clinicians and battered women's advocates are encouraging the diagnosis of PTSD for battered women as the best of the currently available diagnostic options (Browne, 1993; Dutton, 1992a; Saunders, 1992a). There are no conclusive studies on the extent of PTSD among battered women, but the preliminary observation is that it is substantial. Approximately 45% to 55% of small samples (30-60) of battered women from battered women's programs have been diagnosed as having PTSD, according to standardized instruments (Housekamp & Foy, 1991). The percentage climbs to over 75% in studies drawing on open-ended clinical evaluations and women in immediate crisis (Astin, Lawrence, & Foy, 1993).

The symptomatology for a PTSD diagnosis, according to the *Diagnostic Statistical Manual* (APA, 1994), is presented in Figure 4.9. Someone suffering from PTSD typically has avoidance symptoms (e.g., amnesia, dissociative episodes, withdrawal, depression) and intrusive symptoms (explosive anger, flashbacks, anxiety, hyperactivity). PTSD is often very difficult to diagnose, however, especially without extended observation. Symptoms observed out of context may appear very much like another disorder. For instance, a battered woman with PTSD may appear in court as "hysterical" because intrusive symptoms are triggered by the stress, pressures, and fears raised by the court. At another time, a battered woman may be accused of being neglectful of herself as avoidance symptoms appear. These extremes taken separately suggest separate major disorders. These extremes taken together suggest a person with PTSD coping with an unpredictable and threatening environment.

There are some limitations and shortcomings to the PTSD diagnosis, however. PTSD was developed primarily to address the symptoms of Vietnam War veterans. PTSD from woman battering is often more complex

Experience of a distressing event that involved actual or threatened serious injury or death and a response of intense fear, helplessness, or horror.

Traumatic event is persistently reexperienced in at least one of the following ways:

- Recurrent and intrusive distressing recollections of the event
- Recurrent distressing dreams of the event
- Sudden acting or feeling as if the traumatic event were recurring (includes a sense of reliving the experience, illusions, hallucinations, and dissociative [flashback] episodes, even those that occur upon awakening or when intoxicated)
- Intense psychological distress at exposure to events that symbolize or resemble an aspect of the traumatic event, including anniversaries of the trauma

Persistent avoidance of stimuli associated with the trauma or numbing of general responsiveness (not present before the trauma), as indicated by at least three of the following:

- Efforts to avoid thoughts or feelings associated with the trauma
- Efforts to avoid activities or situations that arouse recollections of the trauma
- Inability to recall an important aspect of the trauma (psychogenic amnesia)
- Markedly diminished interest in significant activities
- Feelings of detachment or estrangement from others
- Restricted range of affect, for example, unable to have loving feelings
- Sense of a foreshortened future, for example, does not expect to have a career, marriage, children, or a long life

Persistent symptoms of increased arousal (not present before the trauma) as indicated by at least two of the following:

- Difficulty in falling or staying asleep
- Irritability or outbursts of anger
- Difficulty concentrating
- Hypervigilance
- Exaggerated startle response
- Physiologic reactivity upon exposure to events that symbolize or resemble an aspect of the traumatic event

Duration of the disturbance (symptoms in B, C, D) of at least one month.

Figure 4.9. Criteria for Posttraumatic Stress Disorder

SOURCE: American Psychiatric Association (1994), pp. 209-211. Based on information from the *Diagnostic and Statistical Manual of Mental Disorders,* Fourth Edition. Used by permission.

than PTSD related to war, hostage taking, or terrorism (Campbell, 1993; Warshaw, 1993). Battered women generally experience repeated trauma-tization over an extended period of time rather than have traumatization end abruptly after a military battle or hostage release. The source of the trauma is often continuing; there is current trauma and present danger, rather than a "post" experience. Additionally, battered women are influ-enced by a wider range of interventions and supports, such as shelters and legal advocacy, that mediate their trauma (Astin et al., 1993). Some psychiatrists have argued, therefore, for a more complex form of PTSD that might apply to battered women (see Herman, 1992). A "complex posttraumatic stress disorder" has yet to be included in the *Diagnostic Statistical Manual.*

Another alternative to PTSD is the battered woman syndrome (BWS) (Campbell, 1990; Douglas, 1987; Walker, 1983). BWS is not recognized in the *Diagnostic Statistical Manual* as a formal psychiatric disorder, but approximates the symptomatology of PTSD specific to battered women. It has been used frequently in court cases to interpret the behavior of battered women who kill their partners (Walker, 1992), albeit with some resistance among advocates. Some have argued that BWS tends to pathologize the rational self-defense of battered women (Bowker, 1995), and that BWS works especially against African American women in the courts (Moore, 1994).

BWS may suggest battered women who are weak, crazy, and pow-erless, rather than acting reasonably to defend themselves. The stereo-type of African American women often portrays them as angry and domineering, and consequently courts are reluctant to accept BWS as their defense. BWS encompasses many of the symptoms of PTSD but emphasizes the ongoing battering of women, as opposed to the more general implications of past trauma to male or female victims implied in PTSD. BWS also identifies the sense of "learned helplessness" that is often ascribed to battered women (Campbell, 1990). Learned helpless-ness suggests that women become so emotionally paralyzed by their abuse that they are unable to seek help. BWS neglects the active coping and help seeking of many battered women if they are experiencing PTSD (Bowker, 1993; Campbell, 1990; Gondolf & Fisher, 1988).

Of course, not all battered women suffer from PTSD or BWS. Some of the acute symptomatology is merely a temporary reaction to an intense crisis situation. Battered women are, in fact, known to respond in a diversity of ways to abuse and trauma (Dutton, Perrin, & Chrestman, 1995). Their response may be affected by their personality, social support, abuse history, and previous interventions. Most battered women appear amazingly resilient and strong at times. The reasons and circumstances of a woman's resiliency have not been substantially researched, however. As discussed in Chapter 5, "Recognizing the Strengths of Battered Women," an assessment of a woman's strengths is likely to reveal some positive characteristics of battered women that might otherwise be neglected in more conventional diagnoses. These strengths may also put a different light on a woman's apparent symptoms and contribute to a different psychiatric diagnosis—or no diagnosis at all.

Process

The principal challenge for those in mental health services is to interpret apparent symptoms in the context of abuse and battering. Alternative diagnoses that account for the abuse should be carefully weighed in diagnosing battered women. As suggested above, any initial diagnosis other than PTSD needs to be made cautiously, and potentially detrimental diagnoses need to be avoided.

A clinician might ideally raise several diagnostic possibilities with a client and explain the consequences of each. The client and the clinician might then decide on the initial diagnosis together. This kind of decision process gives some sense of self-determination and validation to the client. It also affords battered women experience that they very much need to offset the degradation and external control that is often a part of their abuse, and helps avoid further traumatization often associated with imposing diagnostic evaluations.

In any case, the identification of abuse should be noted in the Axis IV diagnosis (or V codes). This diagnosis does not qualify as a mental disorder as such, but does indicate a possible stressor contributing to a disorder. It may also be used as a factor in revising a client's major diagnosis in the future. Finally, the strengths developed in coping with battering need to be recognized and affirmed in some way. A clinician might summarize the strengths often associated with battered women and ask a woman which ones she sees in herself. These strengths may be redirected to help battered women heal and reorder their lives (Campbell, 1990; Dutton, 1992b; Gondolf & Fisher, 1988; Rieker & Carmen, 1986).

▪▪ REPORTING AND DOCUMENTATION

Preliminary research on emergency room, substance abuse, and psychiatric records suggests that woman battering is inaccurately or inadequately described in clinical records and reports. For instance, observations of an urban hospital emergency room and record analysis document that woman battering is obscured or omitted in the majority of woman battering cases. Medical staff report explicit information about abuse in only 21% of the identified battered women (Warshaw, 1989). Moreover, there is little mention of treatment or referral for woman battering in the reports. Despite protocol to the contrary, no social work consultation or shelter information was given in over 90% of the cases in one hospital emergency room (Warshaw, 1989). Similarly, less than 5% of the clinical reports mention consultation, referrals, or treatment for battering or abuse among family members in a sample of nearly 400 psychiatric clients (Gondolf, 1990).

In medical settings, clinical reports tend to reflect conversation patterns that systematically exclude or negate topics such as woman battering (Anspach, 1988; Fisher, 1986; Waitzkin, 1989). Reports use mechanisms for discounting social problems, such as depersonalization, passive voice, and account markers. For instance, a clinician may write, "Patient *claims* she was struck by her husband." In a study of a psychiatric diagnostic center, a series of explicitly reported violent incidents was frequently reduced to vagaries: "marital conflict," "history of abusiveness," or "fighting with family members" (Gondolf, 1990; Warshaw, 1993).

Serious incidents of violence also lose their urgency when presented as part of a listing of other social information: "Patient is married, is unemployed, dropped out of school, had previous suicide attempt, and has fights with her husband." Incidents of violence are implicitly explained as a secondary outcome of alcohol abuse or mental disorder, and without indicating the role and responsibility of the perpetrator. For instance, reports note, "The patient was struck by a fist in an intoxicated state," and "The patient has symptoms of a borderline personality disorder and a history of fights with partner." There is no mention of reported violence in one quarter of the cases where violence had been explicitly mentioned by the client during the evaluation interview.

Figure 4.10 lists several of these tendencies in reporting that should be avoided, and offers information that needs to be included in reports

Things to Avoid

- Using vagaries such as "marital conflict," "history of abuse," or "family fights"
- Identifying incidents as part of a list of other social information (e.g., unemployed, previous suicide attempt, dropped out of school, fights with husband)
- Invalidating or diminishing incidents with qualifiers (e.g., "Patient says . . ." "Person claims . . ." "There may be . . .")
- Premature inferences that battering is a symptom of mental disorder or substance abuse (e.g., "The patient was struck in an intoxicated state.")
- Blaming the victim for the abuse (e.g., patient started an argument; patient was drinking)
- Detailing extraneous information that may harm the victim in later custody or court cases
- Culturally, ethically, or racially insensitive remarks or assumptions

Things to Include

- Details of circumstances, tactics, time, place, effect, and injury of battering incidents
- Context of battering incidents, including other forms of nonphysical abuse (e.g., isolation, financial control, intimidation, emotional abuse, financial abuse) and sexual abuse
- Description of the pattern of battering in terms of frequency, duration, cycles, and escalation
- Evidence of dangerousness and lethality risk
- Previous contacts with police, court, clergy, lawyers, mental health services, battered women programs, or friends and relatives about battering
- Recommendations for safety and protection
- Name the perpetrator and state abuse as his responsibility

Figure 4.10. Clinical Records of Woman Battering
SOURCE: American Psychiatric Association (1994), pp. 209-211.

and records. The reports should include details of abuse and battering derived from the abuse history, a lethality checklist, and safety planning. They should explicitly mention the circumstances, tactics, time, place, effect, and injury of battering incidents. The context of the battering incidents, such as nonphysical abuse and sexual abuse, should also be noted. The reports should summarize, as well, a woman's previous informal and formal help seeking, such as contacting friends, calling the police, or going to a shelter. Finally, recommendations for safety and protection, along with referrals and treatment plans to address the woman battering, should be cited.

The failure to note the abuse and battering explicitly may invalidate and disconfirm a battered woman's sense of her abuse and make her reluctant to disclose relevant information in the future (Warshaw, 1989, 1993). Clinical records are also used as the basis of treatment or further evaluations. A woman's abuse history is likely to be neglected or over-looked if it is not explicitly mentioned in the records and plans for treatment and referral are not explicitly outlined (Gondolf, 1990). The records and reports also offer documentation that may help victims obtain additional services, as well as defend themselves in divorce and child custody cases.

Battering cases might also be entered into a computerized record system of battering, similar to that being developed in hospitals for violent cases. Such a record system may be useful in tracking and identifying the reentry of battering cases into social service, clinic, or hospital care. It also can be useful in developing specialized services for battered women and improving the response of mental health services in general. Systematic information is increasingly needed in policy for-mulation and evaluation. Identifying the extent and nature of woman battering may in itself increase clinician awareness and concern.

■■ CONCLUSION

Some very practical measures can be introduced in conventional mental health evaluations to identify battered women and more meaningfully assess their situation. Screening questions about behaviors and effects associated with abuse and follow-up questions that probe the nature, extent, and dynamics of abuse substantially increase the identification of battered women. More elaborate assessment instruments have been developed to establish the severity and type of abuse. Guide questions for assessing a woman's abuse history are also available.

Information on the presence, nature, severity, and history of abuse is essential in responding to battered women in mental health services.

Battered women's advocates strongly urge developing a safety plan with battered women. Safety plans generally identify options that might help interrupt or avoid escalating violence. Such plans usually also outline many commonsense procedures that will help battered women escape a dangerous situation.

The most controversial area in assessing woman battering is deriving an appropriate diagnosis of a woman's mental state. Knowledge of the abuse history can help clinicians better determine to what extent apparent symptoms may be coping tactics or trauma effects. The use of PTSD has become popular in this regard, but battered women respond in a diversity of ways to trauma. Some advocate-clinicians recommend negotiating a diagnosis with a woman client that best represents her evolving symptomology and practical needs.

Advocates and researchers alike recommend enhancing the accounts of woman battering in clinical records. The tendency in clinical records has been to diminish the abuse and violence with neutral terminology (e.g., marital dispute) or cast it as a secondary concern. Details of the abuse, including the extent, severity, and tactics, can help in developing appropriate treatment and in the documentation of violence for other referral sources, especially to the courts. Otherwise, woman battering can easily be lost in the shuffle of mental health services; in the process, women's claims of abuse become unconfirmed and discounted.

▪▪ NOTE

1. To score the ISA, the physical subscale items (ISA-P) need to be calculated separately from the nonphysical subscale items (ISA-NP). (The P and NP items are listed at the bottom of the ISA instrument.) The ISA-P score is computed by multiplying the item score (1-5) by the item weight and then totaling the products for the ISA-P items. (The weights, used to account for varying degrees of severity, appear in parentheses at the end of each item on the instrument.) This sum is then divided by 682, the dividend is subtracted from 1, and the result is multiplied by 25: ISA – P = sum of (P item scores × item weight) ÷ 682 – 1) × 25. The nonphysical or NP score is similarly calculated: ISA – NP = sum of (NP item scores × item weights) ÷ 387 – 1) × 25. These formulas are used to develop a score based on 0 to 100. Higher scores indicate the presence of a greater degree or amount of abuse.

A validation study with 398 university students showed that an ISA-P score of 10 and an ISA-NP cut score of 25 are the best clinical cut scores to minimize false positives and false negatives (Hudson & McIntosh, 1981). For example, the classification error rate for the ISA-P cut score is 9.3% for false positives, 7.8% for false negatives, and 9.3% for the total sample. Conversely, the cut score of 10 for the ISA-P correctly classifies 90.7% of the sample. If a woman has experienced a great deal of nonphysical abuse (ISA-NP score), she is likely to have experienced a great deal of physical abuse (ISA-P score) (r = .86).

Score ranges for various categories of battering (low risk to very high risk) are being developed by the authors of the instrument but remain suspect at this point. The ISA, like other inventories, measures the type of abuse and not necessarily its effect. It is not a predictive instrument as such. That is, it assesses what has been done in the past, which may or may not correlate to the future pattern of abuse. Future abuse is very difficult to predict because of interventions that may preclude abusive behavior and the variety of factors associated with reoffense. It is recommended, therefore, that the scores be used for a relative comparison of degree and amount. The overall severity of physical abuse for someone with a score of 40 is probably twice as severe as someone with a score of 20. (Both scores may be dangerous and harmful to the individual, however.) In addition to the scoring, the items on the instrument might be reviewed to see what actually is being done and with what frequency. This test will help the clinician formulate the pattern of abuse and abuse history. The test scores might also be given to a woman to help her grasp the severity of the abuse.

More information on the scoring options and emerging categories of the ISA may be obtained from Walmyr Publishing Co., P.O. Box 24770, Tempe, AZ 85285-4779 (phone 602-897-1040). This company also sells forms of the ISA and updated scoring mechanisms.

5

Recognizing the Strengths of Battered Women

with Angela Browne, PhD

One of the greatest services mental health clinicians can offer battered women is to identify their strengths—especially because their batterers and often the public in general tend to negate them routinely. By strengths, we mean the qualities that resist attack and defeat and maintain survival and personal growth. An increasing number of social workers, trauma therapists, and resiliency experts are forging a movement of such a strengths assessment (e.g., Cowger, 1994; Goldstein, 1990; Saleeby, 1992; Weick, Rapp, Sullivan, & Kisthardt, 1989). An assessment of strengths, as opposed to one of weakness and deficiencies, helps identify an individual's potential and serves to engage, activate, and empower the individual, according to the proponents of strengths assessment.

Although hundreds of assessment instruments exist for pathology, there remains an absence of instruments to assess the inner strengths of victims and survivors. Much of the instrumentation that may approximate a strengths assessment—methods of coping or assessments of belief systems—are normed on middle-class married couples or college

95

students (e.g., Carver, Scheier, & Weintraub, 1989; Nowotny, 1989; Scheier
& Carver, 1985). Clinical evaluation procedures, moreover, seldom address strengths (Goldstein, 1990). None of the clinical textbooks that we
reviewed explicitly identifies a strengths assessment (Gondolf, 1990).
These texts tend to focus on establishing a diagnosis of mental difficulties
or illnesses.

Advocates in the domestic violence field have worked to emphasize
the strengths of women faced with assault and threat, especially in terms
of their perseverance, courage, and fortitude in coping with abuse (e.g.,
Bowker, 1983; Gondolf & Fisher, 1988). Knowledge of victim and survivor actions reveals the complex coping efforts of women attempting to
survive abuse amid real danger and little effective help or assistance
(Browne, 1987, 1993; Walker, 1984). Advocates and clinicians working in
the domestic violence field have also developed *empowerment* counseling
that attempts to validate and affirm a survivor's feelings, perceptions,
and efforts (Dutton, 1992b; Worell & Remer, 1992).

Empowerment and Strength Approaches

Battered women tend to blame and distrust themselves as a result
of their partner's negating, degrading, and isolating behavior (Browne,
1993; Dutton, 1992b; Koss et al., 1994). In most cases, empowerment
counseling is focused on accepting a woman's feelings, identifying her
immediate needs, alerting her to useful options, and reinforcing her will
to survive (Dutton, 1992b; Worell & Remer, 1992). The principal objective
is to encourage self-determination—that is, to make decisions in one's
best interest. The process of empowerment counseling attempts to enlist
a woman in the assessment process and guide her toward options that
address her needs. This process goes a long way to strengthening a
battered woman, but may not explicitly and systematically assess her
strengths and then build on them. In fact, empowerment may seem to
imply starting from a negative position of "disempowerment" and
weakness, or suggest that the counselor or advocate is stronger or more
competent than the woman. It also may not specifically address the
posttrauma effects associated with physical and sexual assault that mask
strengths in some women (Simon, 1990).

An approach based on the assessment of strengths builds on this
empowerment and survivor work while redressing the shortcomings of
conventional assessment and evaluation procedures (Cowger, 1994;

Goldstein, 1990; Saleebey, 1992). Its most fundamental distinction is that strengths assessment focuses on individual and internal strengths, rather than on pathology and problems, and then works out to the problems of abuse and the effects of trauma (see Browne, 1995a). It assumes strength in even the most devastated survivor or the most troubled current victim of violence, oppression, or degradation. The strengths approach views a victim's or survivor's strengths as basic to her constitution, rather than her past traumas and their sequelae as all encompassing. In discussing this approach, Browne (1995a) contends that a victim or survivor is more than the outcome of physical or sexual violations, even if the abuse started in early childhood and continues into adulthood. The victim is more than the sum of events that have happened to her. The strengths model, in this sense, offers a more complete human picture of an individual, her history, and her potential.

This chapter presents the rationale for recognizing the strengths of battered women and an inventory to assess strengths during mental health evaluations. The first section addresses the concern among many battered women's advocates that symptoms of psychopathology may actually be coping strategies, understandable responses, or necessary compensation for abuse and battering. Women's strengths are often misinterpreted as weaknesses and even illness, but have a different meaning when viewed in the context of woman battering. The second section reviews the assumptions of *survivor theory* as a way to explain why strengths persist or emerge where we might least expect them. A drive toward protection of self and children and the transcendence of the human spirit often provide resiliency amid hardship. The last section outlines specific questions and procedures to identify and explore an individual's strengths. It shows how to assess the relative levels of various strengths, how to apply the strengths to personal difficulties and the effects of trauma, and how to use strengths in assessing abuse and posing treatment.

■■ RECOGNIZING STRENGTHS

The strengths in battered women may sometimes be difficult to identify because they are masked by the debilitating effects of trauma. For instance, women with violent and degrading partners often experience severe low self-esteem, guilt, self-blame, depression, and a sense of

Apparent symptomatology evaluated in the context of abuse may instead be:

- Coping strategies and means of surviving abuse
- Response to women's roles and relationship expectations
- Anxiety over separation from the batterer and uncertainty of the future
- Creative adaptation to posttraumatic stress and trauma in general
- Mechanisms for coping with mental illness and efforts to endure symptoms

Figure 5.1. Redefining Symptoms

extreme vulnerability and futility (Cascardi & O'Leary, 1992). In the past, they have been characterized as suffering from learned helplessness—a kind of "psychological paralysis" that inhibits their response to dangerous situations (Walker, 1979). In a broader context, however, these responses are what one would expect of any trauma survivor (Browne, 1993) and may be a necessary part of the battered woman's healing process (Gondolf & Fisher, 1988). In light of a woman's abuse history, symptoms also may be a kind of coping strategy, an adaptation to relationship expectations. These symptoms may, therefore, be a reflection of strengths, rather than detriments in some cases (see Figure 5.1).

Coping Strategies

One of the particular concerns among battered women's advocates is that mental health clinicians may assess what are essentially coping strategies as symptoms of mental problems or disorders. Certain behaviors, reactions, or characteristics may be ways of enduring inescapable abuse, reducing the level of violence, or protecting children from the abuser. Some battered women may, for example, appear so careless or resigned to the abuse that they are labeled *masochistic* (Caplan, 1985). A battered woman may even prompt imminent abuse from her partner—and thus appear provocative—in order to receive the violence when she is more able to defend herself rather than when she is off guard, asleep, or about to go to work or school. Her actions may also be an attempt to divert her partner from abusing the children. Some women may, moreover, appear careless out of "battle fatigue" or the realization that they cannot do much to stop their partner's violence.

Relationship Expectations

Symptoms associated with a mental disorder might be a manifestation of some other natural response to a woman's role in her relationship. Her depression and self-blame may be related to her effort to maintain the marriage, nurture her family, protect her children, or ease the suffering of her partner. Abuse precipitates a sense of failure to live up to gender or personal expectations in relationships. As in-depth interview studies show (Ferraro & Johnson, 1983; Mills, 1985), battered women tend to blame themselves initially for not being nurturing, supportive, or loving enough to make their marriages or relationships work. Images of the partner as loving or protective, as well as hopes for the relationship in the future, are often shattered when a partner becomes violent. The depression experienced by some battered women may be a form of internalized anger against the batterer. This anger is difficult to express for many women because of the abusive retaliation it may bring, and because women tend to be socialized not to express their anger or rage.

Separation Issues

Some symptoms may be a response to the situation of leaving a batterer or seeking help for the abuse. The depression and guilt of battered women who have fled to shelters may, for instance, be a response to separation. A woman may understandably feel some anxiety about living in an unfamiliar, supervised residence apart from the batterer and her home (Mitchell & Hodson, 1983). Battered women face tremendous uncertainty in separating even temporarily from the batterer. They fear reprisals for leaving, loss of custody of the children, and losing their home and financial support. The unknown of trying to survive on one's own, especially considering the lack of adequate employment or educational opportunities and child care for low-income women, can be as frightening and as daunting as returning to a violent man. Given the rapid escalation in the poverty of women and children in the contemporary United States, returning to the batterer may seem the lesser of the two evils.

The writings about other kinds of survivors appear to support this notion of separation anxiety as an explanation of apparent pathological symptoms. Robert Lifton (1967), well-known for studies on survivors of death camps and nuclear destruction, found that an impaired mourning, psychological numbing, and paranoia may set in as part of a "death spell." In a sense, a battered woman must admit the death of her relationship and, symbolically, the death of her husband. To leave him or seek help is to admit that he is dead to her efforts to change him. Women are left virtually without supports in grieving the loss of their partner, relationship, and home. Although cognitively and clinically we know that the loss of a primary relationship often results in a prolonged period of sadness, women who have left an abusive partner are frequently denied an empathic hearing for their grief. Seen in context, denial, anger, and depression may all be steps in a normal adjustment to loss.

In sum, some symptomatology in battered women may be an adaptation to a situation brought about by a woman's courage to seek help, launch out in the unknown, and survive and better herself. The fear, depression, and guilt associated with separation and loss are understandable and healthy reactions to the changes brought by the aftermath of difficult decisions and the exertion of one's strengths. If women survivors did not exhibit some level of expected emotion for these circumstances, they might be considered naive, uncaring, devoid of affect, or immature.

Posttrauma Effects

Another way to interpret apparent symptomatology is as an understandable response to past trauma—and a creative response at that (Browne, 1993; Carmen, 1995). As discussed in Chapter 4, "Procedures for Assessing Woman Battering," many symptoms ascribed to battered women may in fact be part of a complex posttraumatic stress syndrome, rather than the manifestation of a chronic mental disorder or illness (Dutton, 1992a; Herman, 1992). A person dealing with posttraumatic effects or posttraumatic stress disorder (PTSD) may vacillate between periods of depression, hypervigilance, flashbacks, and amnesia. In the extreme, these symptoms can be disturbing, debilitating, and detrimental. Someone who becomes hypervigilant may overreact to some situations, thus distancing potential supporters or becoming stigmatized by agency officials or the courts as "incompetent." On the other hand, the variety of reactions or "symptoms," at a lower level, can be the body's and mind's way of recovering from stress and protecting oneself from further trauma. An individual may need to grieve, to cry, and to wonder as a way of healing the pain of trauma.

What appears as symptomatology might be more a situational response or adaptation—in this case, to past abusive situations rather than to the present uncertainty of leaving abuse. The symptoms may be normal human responses to trauma as well as part of the healing process. To have endured, coped, and survived previous trauma in itself implies survival strengths worthy of recognition and affirmation (Browne, 1995a). Severe posttraumatic reactions may, of course, warrant psychological counseling and therapy. This therapy ought to acknowledge the situations contributing to the trauma and build on the strengths individuals have developed to deal with them. Several treatment guides for treating the posttraumatic stress of battered women are now available (Dutton, 1992a; Herman, 1992; Koss et al., 1994; Walker, 1994).

Mental Illness

Some battered women do suffer from serious mental problems, either in response to trauma or as part of a chronic mental illness. The recent theories and research on trauma show that a substantial portion of battered women are deeply affected by violence and sexual assault (see Herman, 1992; Koss et al., 1994, for reviews of the research). For some, their sense of self is so extensively damaged through repeated violation, invasiveness, shaming, betrayal, and degradation that they may manifest symptoms of a borderline personality disorder. They may so repress and deny their painful feelings and anger that they exhibit signs of a dissociative disorder—a common response among a wide range of trauma survivors. They may so distort and decontextualize the meanings of their abuse in an attempt to "explain it away" that they seem delusional. Finally, some battered women may get so caught in a cycle of repetitive reenactment of their repressed feelings toward others that they appear impulsive or affectively disordered. The "disconfirmation" of trauma (the effort to negate and avoid trauma), or attempt to anesthetize the pain, may manifest in suicidality, self-mutilation, substance abuse, sexual dysfunction, transient psychoses, eating disorders, and dissociative disorders (Carmen, 1995; Herman, 1992).

Major mental illness may, additionally, accompany the victimization of women and dangerously compound it. The disorientation, lack of self-care, and inappropriate decisions that often accompany mental illness, and the sense of powerlessness and worthlessness frequently associated with being a mentally ill person, make an individual particularly vulnerable to abuse, exploitation, and neglect. Bipolar depression or schizophrenia, for instance, tends to put both women and men at risk for homelessness, drug abuse, severe assault, and HIV infection.

Histories of abuse and trauma remain relevant to even the most chronic major disorders for at least two reasons. First, the major disorders are generally caused or heightened by physical or sexual assault by intimates, particularly that occurring in childhood (see Herman, 1992). Addressing the trauma—and the abuse that contributes to it—can therefore alleviate symptoms of the disorder. Second, mentally ill battered women are very likely to suffer PTSD in response to sexual exploitation, neglect, homelessness, or institutionalization, as well as woman battering. A second diagnosis of PTSD is, therefore, probable and warrants intervention beyond the treatment of the major disorder or illness, according to the recent wave of clinical literature (see Koss et al., 1994).

The greatest challenge for clinicians trained to focus on psychological deficiencies and pathology is to recognize strengths in cases in which chronic mental illness or major mental disorders are apparent. Yet among even the most troubled individuals, there are times of coherence, insight, and courage. A will to survive brings many women with mental illness forward for help. They exert tremendous effort to endure the sometimes punishing symptoms of their mental illnesses. They persevere amid social isolation, meager resources, and—often—ongoing traumatizing experiences.

A movement of "psychiatric survivors" has actively been confirming the tenacious survival strengths of mental patients (Deegan, 1995; Stefan, 1995). Former mental patients turned activists assert that their personal strengths rather than psychiatric treatment, drug therapy, or manipulative counseling are primarily responsible for their recovery from mental illness. They believe that conventional psychiatric treatments negated their strengths and subjugated them as women (e.g., Chamberlin, 1978; Chesler, 1972). To alleviate the suffering and promote the well-being of these survivors, clinicians need to acknowledge the trauma of battered women and recognize their survival strengths.

1. Severe abuse prompts innovative coping strategies from battered women and efforts to seek help. Previous abuse and neglect by help sources lead women to try other help sources and strategies to lessen the abuse. The battered woman, in this light, is a "survivor."

2. The survivor may experience anxiety or uncertainty over the prospects of leaving the batterer. The lack of options, know-how, and finances raises fears about trying to escape the batterer. The battered woman may therefore attempt to change the batterer instead of attempting to leave.

3. The survivor actively seeks help from a variety of informal and formal help sources. There is most often inadequate or piecemeal help giving that leaves the woman little alternative but to return to the batterer. The help seeking continues, however.

4. The failure of help sources to intervene in a comprehensive and decisive fashion allows abuse to continue and escalate. The inadequacy of help sources may be attributed to a kind of learned helplessness experienced in many social services. Service providers feel too overwhelmed and limited in their resources to be effective and therefore do not try as hard as they might.

5. Battered women as survivors of abuse need, most of all, access to resources that enable them to escape the batterer. Community services need to be coordinated to assure the needed allocation of resources and integrated to assure long-term comprehensive intervention.

Figure 5.2. Survivor Theory

■■ TOWARD A SURVIVOR THEORY

How might one account for the strengths among battered women who have been through so much? The converging domestic violence and trauma fields have increasingly explained the strengths among the victimized with what amounts to a survivor theory (Browne, 1993, 1995; Gondolf & Fisher, 1988; Rieker & Carmen, 1986; Walker, 1994). The fundamental assumption is that individuals who are abused or battered have innate strengths and work to change or improve their situation and to protect themselves and their children. They exert a diversity of coping responses in response to the severity and nature of the threat and violence and the extent and kind of support they receive (see Figure 5.2).

Self-Transcendence

The assertions about the survivor strengths of battered women also reflect a more fundamental philosophical assumption about human nature. Survivor theory goes beyond concepts such as assertion, self-actualization, self-determination, and cognitive attribution as demonstrations of strength. It incorporates what Frankl (1959) and others have referred to as *self-transcendence*: yearning for dignity, desire for good, and instinct to stay alive that endure despite one's previous conditioning or present circumstances. Even in the midst of severe psychological impairment, women victims seek help, communicate their hardships, adapt, and push on. In fact, extremely punishing circumstances may activate help seeking, a desperate exertion, or denial of fears and doubts, according to recent research (Gondolf & Fisher, 1988).

This is not to say that one should expect battered women or other survivors of abuse and misfortune to bounce back on their own. Rather, by offering respectful understanding and useful supports, clinicians can facilitate an individual's realization of her inner strength, worth, and resiliency. Clinicians or helpers have the opportunity to affirm and accentuate this potential in others by displaying it in themselves. As helpers express resiliency, a positive outlook, and determination, rather than succumbing to a negative or cynical outlook so prevalent in social services today, then those they reach out to are more likely to recognize and act on their strengths.

Implications for Assessment

The approach to assessing strengths is more than a matter of what some advocates refer to as *reframing*. Reframing suggests reinterpreting symptomatic behaviors in a different light to see them as strengths rather than as weaknesses. The strengths approach, instead, broadens the focus to include strengths that are inherently present but often overlooked in the preoccupation with pathology. A woman's depression might, for instance, be genuinely debilitating. Rather than attempt to redefine the depression, the strengths approach accentuates the behaviors that have been a positive force in the woman's life. What about the persistence in seeking help amid fear and uncertainty? What about getting up after being knocked down so many times? What about the woman's care and protection of her children amid feelings of sadness and grief? The mental health clinician should screen for mental problems, especially those associated with abuse and trauma, but in the process, shift to the strengths that sustain the individual and portend progress.

The strengths approach is not meant to be a technique such as brief cognitive therapy or solution-oriented therapy. These therapies tend to focus on immediate possibilities, resolutions, and answers to problems rather than their origins or underlying dynamics. The strengths approach acknowledges trauma as a fundamental issue for many battered women. Knowing a person's abuse history is essential in identifying and appreciating a woman's strengths. In a sense, the abuse history is proof of one's strengths, because strength is defined as "the power to resist an attack, strain, or stress." On the other hand, the strengths approach is not analytical or emotive therapy for trauma and pain. It attempts to identify the personal resources to deal with abuse and trauma, rather than dwell on what is painful and hopeless and inadvertently reinforce a preoccupation with negative outcomes.

∷ STRENGTHS INVENTORY

Some formal procedure to assess individual strengths in victims and survivors more systematically would be helpful to both clinicians and clients (Browne, 1995a). It would offer mental health clinicians a more complete picture of a woman in the context of past traumas and help in strengthening and guiding clients in present circumstances. It would also provide a positive affirmation to a woman and, in the process, counter the labeling or stigma typically encountered when assessment focuses on identifying pathology. A strengths assessment might, furthermore, offset clinician-client interactions that retraumatize or devalue women and survivors. It recognizes the woman as an "expert" and a full participant in a positive process of identifying and then building on her strengths.

A strengths assessment might be conducted through a kind of inventory of self-perceived strengths (see Figure 5.3). (The following assessment procedure was conceived and developed by Angela Browne; see Browne, 1995a.) The first step is a deliberate identification of strengths. This process can be made explicit with a bar graph that establishes a bar for each identified strength. This graph then becomes a central reference point throughout the intervention process. Each bar is elevated to show

- Conduct an inventory of personal strengths
- Prompt with strengths associated with survivors
- Graph the relative level of the identified strengths
- Compare current strengths levels to past levels
- Apply strengths to difficulties and problems related to abuse
- Explore painful and problematic effects of trauma
- Use strengths to activate, implement, and sustain treatment and safety plans

Figure 5.3. Strengths Assessment

its level in a woman's personal experience at that time. The bar graph is not intended to compare an individual with other people or other groups. Rather, it should reflect an ongoing process of identification, focus, and exploration for a particular person. For example, as more strengths are identified or particular strengths are enhanced, bars can be added or existing ones expanded. A clinician also shares with a client the strengths that she or he sees in the client. The clinician might suggest some of the strengths other women in similar situations have demonstrated (see Table 5.1). The strengths of women who have survived severe trauma often include perseverance, humor, spirituality, endurance, loyalty, love for others, and connection with others. Many survivors display an ability to affiliate—however temporarily—with others, despite the rejection, hardship, and isolation they have experienced (Browne, 1995a, 1995b).

Identifying Strengths

Once an initial set of strengths has been identified, the chart should be used to assess the relative level of the identified strengths. The mental health clinician might ask the following questions:

- Which of these strengths are strongest right now? Why?
- What is the least used and least active strength at the moment? Why?
- When are you most likely to use certain strengths? Why then?
- What other strengths would you like to draw on and when?

TABLE 5.1 Characteristics of Battered Women

Ascribed Weaknesses	Probable Strengths
Helplessness	Coping
Depression	Persistence
Fearfulness	Courage
Distrust	Loyality
Denial	Nurturing
Repression	Protective of children
Delusion	Perseverance
Disassociation	Endurance
Distress	Humor
Highly emotional	Creativity

- Where did these strengths come from? How did you develop them?

A clinician might next prompt the individual to compare her current strengths levels, represented on the graph, to the past levels:

- What used to be your greatest strength or strengths? How has that changed? Why?
- What strengths were there in childhood, in teenage years, on the streets, in the home?
- What form are your past strengths in now? Are they buried or dormant? Are you using them in different ways?
- How might you refind, reactivate, and reuse these past strengths?
- What might you do to elevate that area?

Applying Strengths

A clinician can then help a woman apply her strengths to difficulties and problems related to past or current abuse:

- Which of your strengths might be most useful in helping to protect yourself? In what particular ways might you use them to increase your safety?

- Which strengths might lead you out of fear and suffering? How might that work?
- Which strengths might be used to enhance the quality of your life, the lives of your children?
- To what other obstacles or goals might you apply each particular strength?

Once an explicit and ongoing inventory of strengths has begun, the clinician then has an affirmative basis to move on to the painful and problematic effects of trauma. Clinicians thus guide the survivor in the application of identified strengths to deeper psychological effects of trauma, as well as to obstacles and dangers present in external circumstances.

- What internal barriers or obstacles are there to the application of strengths (e.g., posttrauma effects such as substance abuse, a sense of futility, depression)?
- What comes between your strengths and your desire to use them in the world (e.g., scary ex-partner, nonresponsive legal system, lack of employment or shelter)?
- Which of the barriers facing you are yours to deal with or confront, and which ones can you simply drop or step around?
- How can you push the remaining barriers aside—part the curtain, so to speak—between you and where you want to go in the world?

Lastly, the graph or strengths inventory can be used to help activate, implement, and sustain treatment and safety plans.

- Which of these strengths should you focus on now to offset the most acute, the most immediate, the most endangering, and the most painful effects of abuse?
- What combination of these growing strengths can you apply to particularly resistant effects, problems, or obstacles?
- Which of your strengths will help you follow through with your plans, do the best thing for yourself, and feel good about yourself?
- What sources, places, situations, or people can help you revitalize or nurture these strengths?

■ CONCLUSION

Mental health clinicians tend to focus mental health assessment on problems and pathology—on both the traumas that befall a survivor and the initial and long-term effects of those traumas. An individual's strengths are usually overlooked or mentioned only tangentially in the process. Survivors of abuse are consequently cast as primarily deficient, damaged, or disordered. Little specific or ongoing attention is given to internal or implicit strengths, how to assess them, and how to build on them to refocus and enhance a survivor's life.

Assessing strengths in battered women presents an important challenge, with clear implications for intervention and treatment. To identify and accentuate strengths in even the most severely abused and traumatized person, clinicians might do the following:

1. Make an identification of strengths as a starting point in their assessments of and interventions with victims and survivors.
2. Develop assessment instruments and protocols that can identify strengths with the level of detail and sophistication with which clinicians now attempt to assess mental disorders. These instruments need to be applicable across categories of persons, experiences, and circumstances.
3. Use the identification of strengths in a conscious collaboration with victims and survivors to negate posttrauma effects and to frame positive responses and directions.
4. Communicate information on the strengths of victims and survivors to other service providers or referrals as actively as clinicians now communicate information on the negative outcomes of abuse and trauma.

Returning to strengths as a central reference point is, in itself, therapeutic. It avoids deepening the trauma that often results from an unremitting focus on bad outcomes. In assessing the strengths of battered women, clinicians also affirm women's potential and more accurately reflect their full humanity.

PART III

Other Considerations in Assessment

6

Appreciating Diversity
Among Battered Women

Differences and Stereotypes

The image of battered women is becoming more diverse and complex. As services and outreach have increased over the years, so has the knowledge about the backgrounds and experiences of the women being identified as battered (Koss et al., 1994). Various groupings of women have also emerged to help clarify the special needs and circumstances of battered women from different backgrounds. African American, Hispanic, Asian, Jewish, immigrant, lesbian, and disabled women, for instance, certainly have many issues in common as battered women, but also have been affected by different levels of resources, discrimination, and mobility. They also may have different constrictions and expectations in their relationships.

Women of color may be especially reluctant to seek or mistrustful of seeking mainstream clinical or legal assistance. A Spanish-speaking woman who is immigrating from Mexico might be reluctant to report abuse for fear of losing services or being deported, and may be reluctant to offer details of her abuse for fear of being misunderstood or discriminated against. It is therefore important to consider the particular cultural,

113

racial, and personal differences among women when attempting to identify and assess battering.

Unfortunately, efforts to distinguish the diversity of battered women present some shortcomings of their own. Many of our notions about battered women are based on clinical samples of women that do not represent the diversity of battered women found in the population at large (Campbell, Campbell, King, Parker, & Ryan, 1994). The clinical samples are more likely to comprise women who have some confidence in human services, access to the services, and experience using them. Women of color have been compared to white middle-class women. Consequently, they tend to be characterized in terms of "deficits"—what they lack in terms of education, income, or housing—instead of in terms of their unique strengths (Browne, 1995b; Urquiza, Wyatt, & Root, 1994). As reactions to the O. J. Simpson trial dramatically demonstrate, women of different races, even with similar social and economic status, may have very different perceptions about what is just, appropriate, or necessary.

The recent scholarship on women has exposed that even the more grounded cultural, ethnic, and racial distinctions may be stereotypic (e.g., Crenshaw, 1994). Racial experiences may vary according to one's class, language, or educational opportunities. Women of color may have assimilated or rejected the dominant culture to varying degrees and at different times and in different situations. They may respond to certain expectations at work, another set at home, and a different set with family, all of which may change at different stages of life. Race or ethnicity form only a part—albeit an influential one—of a complex matrix of social circumstances. Battered women—and women in general—are constantly negotiating differences in age, employment, class background, immigration status, religious background, sexual preference, and parenting roles (Crenshaw, 1994). In short, battered women do not fit into neat categories of race, class, or some other social circumstance.

In sum, clinicians need first to be alert to racial and ethnic differences that affect the assessment of woman battering. They also need to go beyond those racial and ethnic differences to make sure they do not become a stereotype in themselves. The prevailing differences become an outline of what to explore, rather than a destination in themselves. This chapter attempts to summarize prevailing racial and ethnic differences that warrant consideration in assessing woman battering. These

TABLE 6.1 Some Considerations for Racial and Ethnic Diversity

Considerations	Racial/Ethnic Grouping				
	African American	Latino	Native American	Asian	Immigrant
Abuse issues	Highest homicide rate Neighborhood violence	Highest incidence of woman abuse Duration generally longer	Relatively new problem Counter to traditions	Lowest incidence Military/mail-order brides	Previous trauma and violence
Cultural attitudes	Emotional expression Aggression defense Protective of man Mistrust of police	Machismo/marinism Sympatica relations Family loyalty Fear of deportation	Deference to authority Less competitiveness Despair and depression Suspicion of white ways	Perseverance/fate Anonymity/privacy	PTSD symptoms Religious taboos against criticizing relationship Cultural neglect of battering
Social circumstances	Family nurturers Sole providers Substandard housing Violent neighborhoods Erosion of services Racial conflicts	Language barriers Strong extended family Family support/dependence Uncertain immigration status Hostility toward immigrants	High alcohol use and despair Shared residence Collective subsistence Use of traditional medicine Historical subjugation	Language and conceptual differences Dependence on family-based business Isolation from family support Eastern medicine and health	Previous repression or persecution Intragroup differences and rivalries Little familiarity with services

NOTE: This table represents an example of the kind of considerations that may emerge from working with a diversity of clients and collaboration with community groups. The ideal would be for clinicians to develop their own outline of considerations through the process of assessing battered women and their own involvement in the community. Otherwise, special issues, attitudes, and circumstances can easily become another stereotype rather than additional insight.

115

Cultural Characteristics
- Attention to nonverbal gestures and styles
- Accommodation of non-Standard English, dialects, and different speech patterns
- Response to subtle behavioral cues and gestures
- Conducting broad social histories that account for social circumstances
- Recognizing metaphoric and indirect questioning

Social Circumstances
- Collaboration with paraprofessionals and community workers
- Consultation with ethnically diverse staff
- Coordination with specialized advocates
- Consideration of the limits to police and court options
- Identifying social and kinship networks for support
- Contacting church organizations, relief agencies, legal services, immigration counselors
- Advocating for income supports, housing, and child care for poor women

---

Figure 6.1. Clinical Responses to Racial and Ethnic Diversity

considerations suggest some of the issues likely to emerge through working more extensively with a diversity of battered women and their respective communities (see Table 6.1).

Certain cultural attitudes may make it difficult for women to reveal or discuss being battered or abused. Social circumstances or family structure make it particularly difficult for some women to respond to safety recommendations or referrals (see Figure 6.1). The prevailing differences for several racial and ethnic groupings are presented below, followed by the implications of these differences for assessing and responding to women in mental health settings.

The increased racial and ethnic sensitivity in the United States makes such an undertaking difficult and at the same time emphatically necessary (Urquiza et al., 1994). The diversity within racial and ethnic groupings sometimes blurs generalizations about one group or another. At the same time, group tendencies need to be acknowledged and appreciated to accommodate a variety of people. As many battered women's advocates suggest, what ultimately may be needed is a genuine and open listening to the life stories of battered women. An appreciation of the social circumstances, diverse experiences, and unique attitudes of individual women can help clinicians grasp the social dimension of what is presented as a clinical problem. The objective, as suggested throughout this book, is to see woman battering from the perspective of the women—in the broader social context, which includes the fear and the consequences associated with abuse.

Current Approaches

In addressing racial and ethnic differences, clinicians attempt to draw on what might be considered three levels of response. Numerous manuals and guidebooks have been developed to instruct primarily clinicians and social workers of European descent about how to recognize and respond to racial and ethnic differences among clients and patients (e.g., Amoja Three Rivers, 1990; Lum, 1992; Ponterotto, Casas, Suzuki, & Alexander, 1995; Proctor & Davis, 1994; Sue & Sue, 1990). Some manuals appear to emphasize the need to become more aware of and sensitive to culturally based attitudes and interactions. Other manuals address the importance of clinicians' collaboration with professionals from diverse backgrounds to ensure a broader perspective. Still others point to making clinical practice more open to and involved in the community it attempts to serve.

The first approach is to increase clinicians' awareness of the experiences and circumstances of clients from diverse backgrounds with the hope of establishing more empathy and sensitivity. Clinicians need to be sensitive to culturally based communication styles, dialects, and gestures, as well as to different values and worldviews. Appreciating this sort of diversity can help clinicians solicit more meaningful information, interpret symptoms more accurately, and respond more appropriately and effectively. This sensitivity can also help avoid misinterpreting or misdiagnosing a client's behaviors. For instance, culturally based deference or perseverance may be mistaken for symptoms of dependent or disassociative disorders.

Some manuals argue that this sort of racial and ethnic sensitivity is more than a product of training or instruction and therefore requires life experience and community involvement. Our own biases and prejudices are often so ingrained that they are difficult to recognize and require more than sensitivity to surmount. The need is to collaborate, or at least consult, with clients and coworkers of diverse backgrounds in assessing different kinds of battered women. Advocates from different racial backgrounds may be needed to help clinicians check their biases or prejudices, as well as to help achieve rapport with hard-to-reach or mistrustful clients. In sum, clinicians need to access and build on the "lived" expertise of those from backgrounds other than their own to respond appropriately to the diversity of battered women.

A third and more demanding approach is to recognize the social and political conditions that underlie apparent racial differences. Programs and clinics may themselves appear racially biased or unresponsive to someone of color (Flaskerud, 1986; Neighbors, 1984). Numerous studies have noted the more "personalistic culture" of many racial and ethnic neighborhoods (Gondolf, 1983). Residents of such neighborhoods are more likely to rely on personal reputation, interpersonal networks, and face-to-face familiarity than on professionals, impersonal services, and procedural transactions. These residents' marginal status may also contribute to their being suspicious or wary of some clinicians or professional services. This is especially the case given that women of color from lower-income communities are likely to end up in public facilities with lower standards of care and regimented environments (Center for Mental Health Services, 1995). Mental health treatment is therefore viewed by some women as a means of control for being different or punishment for being poor.

From this perspective, mental health services may need to decentralize and integrate more directly into the community they wish to serve, much as the community mental health movement of past decades attempted to do (Rappaport, 1977). More paraprofessionals and community outreach workers are needed to build linkages within the community. These linkages would help raise the visibility, trust, and respect that contribute to the disclosure essential in assessing woman battering. Many battered women's programs grew out of a community-based, grassroots effort. Consequently, women's advocates are often familiar with this kind of community outreach and the racial and ethnic issues that surround it. Battered women's advocates from these programs may, therefore, be able to offer assistance and support for mental health clinicians attempting to do the same.

■■ AFRICAN AMERICAN WOMEN

Considerations

African American women are more likely to be beaten by their partners than women of other ethnic groups (Cazenave & Straus, 1979), regardless of income level or drinking behavior (Neff, Holamon, & Schluter, 1995). They also are more likely to be killed by their partners (O'Carroll & Mercy, 1986). African American women of lower socioeconomic status who have been battered are more likely than middle-class white women to need extensive services and support. Government cutbacks and racial discrimination have, of course, limited the availability of services particularly to inner-city residents (Browne, 1995b). African American women who do gain access to services are sometimes inadvertently labeled as *bad* victims who may seem less worthy of services (Loseke, 1992). Clinicians may see some of the women's survival and coping efforts as a lack of the compliance or docility that they tend to associate with "good" victims.

On the surface, African American women who are battered may appear to be more assertive, more confident, and more positive about themselves, and as a result seemingly more resilient (Coley & Beckett, 1988). Some counselors have noted the greater range of emotional self-expression in the African American community—what has sometimes been referred to as *soulfulness*. Some African American women may, therefore, respond to their batterers with outrage or total desperation. They may have been aggressive toward their partner in an effort to deal with the abuse themselves (Neff et al., 1995). Consequently, clinicians sometimes dismiss African American women as antisocial or "just violent" people (Campbell et al., 1994).

This apparent assertiveness and resiliency may reflect the coping skills that many African American women have developed to deal with discrimination, difficult living conditions, and violence in their neighborhoods (Sullivan & Rumptz, 1994). In many cases, aggressiveness is a survival strategy of last resort. There is a sense that "I can't count on anybody else to help me. I have to do it myself." African American women in lower-income neighborhoods are generally responsible for taking care of the family, arranging for public assistance or obtaining income, and providing emotional support and nurturing for their family.

African American scholars note that the problems of African American women are more complex than what may appear in their overt behavior (Crenshaw, 1994; Richie, 1996). Battered African Americans are often caught between a sense that they have to "take care of the situation" themselves and feeling ready and eager to do whatever it takes to stop it. They might call the police or leave temporarily, but they may be reluctant to send their batterer to jail or "ruin" his life with a court case. They are likely to feel protective of the man because of the discrimination and "hard times" he has faced, and obligated to support and assist him emotionally to preserve some sense of family. An African American batterer may appear to be a victim himself—of life on the streets, discrimination in getting a job, or reactions from police and the courts. Batterers often coerce their female partners into criminal activities— theft, drug use, prostitution—that complicate the woman's life even more. The women comply with the men out of fear of retaliation, a sense of loyalty to their partners, or a need to support their family. Seeking help for abuse could expose a woman's criminal past, as well as lead to more serious punishments for the man.

African American women who are battered may, furthermore, experience a kind of "triple jeopardy." Besides being abused and facing discrimination, they are also more likely than other battered women to be entrapped by poor living situations. They are more likely to be living below poverty, to be unemployed or sole providers, to have less access to services and care, and to have more children living with them. They also tend to be at greater risk for disease and accidents—and other health problems (Gordon-Bradshaw, 1988). In sum, African American women who are battered are likely to need numerous resources—medical and mental health services, substance abuse treatment, child care services, income support and financial support, job training and placement, and improved housing (Sullivan & Rumptz, 1994).

African American women are the least likely to have access to these resources, however. The erosion of community services in many inner-city neighborhoods leaves many women on long waiting lists, settling for services of lower quality or resigning themselves to no services at all. Their mistrust of the criminal justice system and courts limits yet another option for assistance or intervention. It is very difficult for them to leave their batterers or establish a sense of safety if they do. As a result, poor African American women, and for that matter women of color generally, may feel entrapped in a chaotic home life sustained by substandard and crowded housing and crime-infested and often violent neighborhoods. They have few safeguards against violence in general and have few reliable resources or services to help them (Hawkins, 1987). As a result, their assertive coping may easily switch to despair and frustration—resignation or anger—or some combination of these.

Clinical Responses

Advocates offer several responses to the unique circumstances of many African American women. Clinicians need to be especially alert not to be distracted by initial appearances of either bold assertiveness or hopeless despair. These emotions in themselves are not likely to capture complex social circumstances that entrap many African American women (Bell, 1991). Given the possibility of racial suspicion or caution, clinicians might also pay special attention to nonverbal communication and gestures for hints of problems that need to be explored (Coley & Beckett, 1988).

Consultation with African American staff or advocates may help in interpreting complex cases and building rapport with African American clients. Aggressive outreach through community organizations and paraprofessionals may assist in building familiarity with and respect for mental health services and contribute to greater trust and disclosure on the part of African American women. Some battered women's programs, for instance, have used paraprofessionals in public housing as a way to reach out to battered women of different races. Mental health services might also enlist black leaders and organizers to guide them in dispersing services and establishing links to the community.

Clinicians need to be especially alert to the limitations in some safety planning ideas. Strategies that involve police protection or recommendations to leave one's residence may be problematic for many African American women. Clinicians might help women identify social and kinship networks that could offer temporary shelter or child care. Clinicians may also need to consider the woman's immediate resource and survival needs that may put her at risk or inhibit safety plans. Women with housing, income, and health problems may especially benefit from a battered women's advocate or agency social worker. In sum, a more comprehensive social history and more extensive intervention may be necessary.

■■ LATINA WOMEN

Considerations

Latina women generally bear a set of cultural characteristics and social circumstances that may make them particularly vulnerable to abuse and battering and yet hesitant to disclose or discuss their situations. According to incidence studies, woman battering among Latina women in the United States may be greater than that of Anglo women, but not greater than that of African American women (Kantor, Jasinski, & Aldarondo, 1994; Neff et al., 1995; Sorenson & Telles, 1991). Battered Latina women in shelters are likely to have experienced a longer duration of abuse, be married at a younger age, have larger families, and stay in relationships longer (Gondolf, Fisher, & McFerron, 1991). Sociologists have attributed the levels and extent of abuse to the "tapestry of Latino culture" that allows for male exploits while encouraging a strong family structure (Perilla, Bakerman, & Norris, 1994).

The most common characteristic associated with the battering of Latina women is the heightened gender messages in the form of *machismo* and *marinism*. Machismo (supporting male bravado and dominance), and marinism (supporting female submission and doting) are associated with higher levels of depression, lower self-esteem in women, and more extensive abuse among women (Perilla et al., 1994). (Some advocates argue that machismo and marinism may be ethnocentric stereotypes imposed by Anglos, but they are recurring topics in Latino cultural studies that warrant at least some consideration.) Cultural anthropologists also point to *simpatico* as a cultural script emphasizing smooth and pleasant social relationships. The empathy associated with maintaining relationships may be manifest in a more laissez-faire and less willful response to others, rather than the hurried and imposing drive of many Anglos. As a result, some Latina women who are battered may be reluctant to act quickly and decisively on their own behalf.

Latina women are also likely to have substantial ties to their extended family, with deep feelings of loyalty, reciprocity, and solidarity and adherence to rigidly defined sex roles. A strong Catholic tradition reinforces the allegiance to a strong family structure for many Mexican women (Torres, 1991). As a result, many Latina women may be inclined to forgo outside support and formal services and turn instead to friends and family in times of need.

This family support can, of course, be a tremendous strength in some cases, but it also can confine some women to unsafe relationships.

These cultural tendencies vary with acculturation, education level, immigration status, and finances. Interestingly, recent research suggests that acculturation to American society may bring a different set of issues to Latina women that actually increases the chances of woman battering (Kantor et al., 1994; Sorenson & Telles, 1991). The decrease in social support and a clash of values that often accompanies acculturation appear to increase the likelihood of wife abuse among Latino families (Kantor et al., 1994). There are, as well, significant cultural differences among Latina women, who represent as many as 32 different countries with multiple ethnic and class compositions (Marin & Marin, 1991).

The most difficult circumstance facing many Latina women remains their immigration status (Santiago & Morash, 1994). Because of the increasing discrimination against and even hostility toward Latino immigrants, Latina women are reluctant about seeking help and bringing public attention to themselves. Even women with U.S. citizenship are substantially affected by the controversies mounting around immigration. Latina women often feel reluctant to solicit aid for other Latina women, because the aid may expose their lack of documentation and create legal problems. It is difficult, moreover, for many Latinos to decipher the many shifts and stipulations of immigration policy. They are left to play it cautious even when they have rightful citizenship. Disclosing battering could lead to investigations that expose grounds for their or their partner's deportation. Battered Latina women also report that their batterers often threaten to have them deported if they report woman battering.

Clinical Responses

Advocates recommend several additional steps to ensure appropriate assessment and response to Latina women on a personal and social level. On a personal level, clinicians need to pay special attention to the possible reluctance of Latina women to report woman battering. This may be related to the depression some Latina women experience in response to the confining gender roles and family expectations they experience (Santiago & Morash, 1994). Social sanctions also inhibit disclosing woman abuse. In the woman's eyes, reporting woman abuse may violate loyalty to her family and risk disgrace within her community. She is also likely to fear legal problems, loss of services, or deportation.

It may be particularly useful, therefore, to develop an in-depth social history that identifies a woman's family ties, allegiances, and dependence and any perceived or actual threats to her immigration status. Advocates caution, however, against probing into actual documentation, because the topic is likely to raise suspicion and distance with Latina women. The clinician, in the process, might attempt to identify family members who could serve as positive and protective support for the woman and services within the Latino community for women with particular status or needs. Many communities have alternative services for Latina and immigrant women, including church organizations, relief agencies, legal services, and specialized domestic violence advocates. Because of the fears and barriers faced by many Latina women, clinicians may need to place or connect women with the appropriate services actively, rather than simply make a referral (Bonilla-Santiago, 1996).

In sum, clinicians may need to conduct a more comprehensive social history with Latina women and to conduct more outreach to ensure the women's safety and support. Collaboration with specialized legal services and victim services for Latinas may be an essential step in reaching this goal. Ultimately, clinicians may need to be involved more fully with the issues that community-based organizations and advocacy groups are attempting to address. The problems associated with immigration status, access to services, and cultural identity have a great influence on the well-being of battered Latina women, as well as Latinos in general.

▣ NATIVE AMERICAN WOMEN

Considerations

Woman battering, and family violence in general, is a relatively new phenomena among Native Americans (Chester, Robin, Koss, Lopez, & Goldman, 1994). Traditional values of balance and harmony rooted in the reverence for a mother figure forbade woman battering. Many Native American tribes enacted strong sanctions against anyone who abused a woman or child as a desecration of a sacred bond. A violation of a woman was feared within some tribes, because of the woman's powers regarding life and death. The discrimination, living conditions, and alcohol abuse of modern times have unfortunately offset this cultural tradition. An estimated 80% of Native Americans in urban areas are purported to have a history of family violence (Chester et al., 1994), and the rate may be nearly as high on many reservations or rural native communities. Variations, of course, exist across the more than 500 recognized tribal identities and among those who migrate between the reservation or tribal life and urban areas.

Several cultural values may impede the identification of woman battering or contribute to misunderstandings in assessing the abuse that does surface. Less competitiveness and individualism is sometimes mistaken as lack of initiative or helplessness. The collective spirit of many Native Americans is often manifested in shared residences, moving among relatives' homes, and joining together in fishing, gathering, and hunting activities (Allen, 1990). Separating oneself from a batterer may therefore be extremely difficult and impractical in some Native American communities. There is, moreover, a sense of deference among many Native Americans that may appear to clinicians as withholding or resistance. The reliance on traditional medicine may also contribute to some Native American women's being reluctant to rely on conventional mental health services or confide in mental health clinicians.

Alcohol abuse appears to have a central role in woman battering among Native Americans regardless of tribal affiliation or place of residence. Nearly all battering cases among Native Americans involve alcohol abuse, as opposed to 30% to 60% in the general population (Powers, 1988). The high levels of alcohol abuse—four times the rate of other minority groups—reflect the poor living conditions, lack of employment, extreme subjugation, and history of discrimination that beset many Native American communities. Higher levels of depression and outright despair accompany much of the alcoholism and make the battering even more problematic (Chester et al., 1994). It may therefore be especially difficult to interrupt the battering without dealing not only with the prevalence of alcohol abuse, but also with the underlying despair and the accompanying living conditions of many Native Americans.

Clinical Responses

Advocates working with Native American women pose a number of responses to their special circumstances. One is for clinicians to exercise patience with different speech patterns and body language that may be an expression of a Native American's deference toward others or her caution about conventional health methods. Clinicians might allow for longer moments of silence and more understated problems. Direct and immediate questions about woman battering or alcohol abuse may be seen as intrusive and discourteous, so indirect ways of exploring problems might be used. Metaphors and stories, for instance, often prove to be helpful ways to raise issues with Native Americans steeped in oral history. Clinicians might, furthermore, use alcohol abuse as a cue for woman battering, given the especially high association between alcohol abuse and woman battering among Native Americans. Women are more likely to disclose alcohol abuse as a problem than battering.

The special cultural and social circumstances of Native American women raise additional considerations for responding to battering. One is the need to pose intervention for alcohol abuse as well as the battering, and in a way that does not put the women at further risk. Treatment strategies that employ family confrontation of the alcoholic are in general ill-advised in woman battering cases, but are especially inappropriate among Native Americans (Chester et al., 1994). The possibility of shared residences and collective activities needs to be weighed in formulating safety plans. Battered women at extreme risk may need to be transported to other communities to ensure their safety. Tribal groups, councils, and services may be able to offer local support and protection. An increasing number of Native American services are emerging to deal with alcohol abuse and family problems, including woman battering. Most of these appeal to native traditions and spiritual perspectives for strength, direction, and healing. To make a substantial difference, mental health and woman battering interventions need ultimately to align with community development efforts that address the underlying resource and discrimination problems that beset Native American clients and build on their traditional and spiritual strengths.

■■ ASIAN WOMEN

Considerations

Much less is known about woman battering among diverse groups of Asian women than women of other racial and ethnic backgrounds.

Little specific research has been done on the topic, and what has been done suggests a lower level of woman battering among Asians (Koss et al., 1994). Asian community centers, however, report extensive and complicated abuse against Asian women in the United States (Jang, 1994). There are increasing concerns, for instance, that military brides or mail-order brides are likely to be abused and battered. These women tend to be especially vulnerable because they are isolated from family support, fear deportation, and are financially dependent on their partners. In immigrant couples, the woman may be dependent on the man because he is more likely to speak English than the woman. Family life, especially for Asian immigrants, is usually organized around a family business. These arrangements increase a woman's dependence on her husband and relatives and may make it impractical for her to leave or report abuse (Huisman, 1996).

The role of women in most Asian cultures has been particularly confining, according to some international women's experts (Ho, 1990). A tradition of perseverance and respect for fate has helped women bear harsh living conditions and oppressive societies. This tradition has also made it difficult for some Asian women to challenge and respond to being battered. A concern for anonymity and privacy often contributes to hiding problems and avoiding intervention. As a result, divorce is much less common among Asian women than other racial or ethnic groupings (Ho, 1990). The women are also likely to subscribe to Eastern medicine and concepts of health and therefore are more likely to resist or be suspicious of mental health clinicians who are trying to help them. Health services in general are very unlikely to have Asian interpreters or specialized programs for Asians that might bridge some of the resistance (Sue & Sue, 1990).

Clinical Responses

Advocates suggest at least two major considerations in assessing woman battering among Asian women. One is to pay special attention to cues of violence and respectfully probe those cues for more information. As with women of some other ethnic groups, Asian women, especially Asian immigrant women, may be hesitant to disclose battering or abuse because of their cultural views about privacy, perseverance, and self-restraint or their fears about their immigration status. Advocates encourage clinicians to avoid dependent personality and disassociative diagnoses that may be based on behaviors related to culturally based deference rather than pathology (Ho, 1990).

Clinicians need also to investigate the extended family situation of Asian women and the financial dependence of women on family members (Huisman, 1996). The economic structure of the woman's family or her dependence on a military or mail-order husband may limit her options and ability to seek safety. The family may in other cases be the best source for support and assistance. A clinician may be able to identify one or two supportive kin that a battered woman can turn to for help even amid a confining or abusive family. In some communities, specialized services for Asian women may consult on cases or assist with case management.

▙ IMMIGRANT WOMEN

Considerations

The numbers of women immigrating from a variety of countries and societies raise many of the same concerns mentioned for Hispanic and Asian women. It is important to emphasize, however, that women who are migrants or immigrants have an additional set of challenges facing them regardless of their race or ethnicity (Huisman, 1996). They may be fleeing political repression, religious persecution, or economic devastation in their native countries. An increasing number are refugees from civil wars and strife. They often carry scars of abuse and violence from the hands of soldiers, rebels, or even those who arrange for their transport. They may not only have been traumatized by violence, battering, and rape but also have been numbed by it in a way that complicates assessment. Acute posttraumatic stress, as well as cultural issues, may be at play (Sue & Sue, 1990).

Because of their language and cultural differences, immigrant women may not be able to understand our concepts of woman abuse, or mental health for that matter (Sue & Sue, 1990). Western service providers may have difficulty understanding how a woman feels and the circumstances of her abuse even if they do understand the concepts. Immigrant women simply may not know the terms or misunderstand mainstream definitions. Even native translators may miss a great deal because of tremendous diversities within ethnic, racial, and national groups. There may, in fact, be inhibiting intragroup, tribal, religious, or ethnic conflict or rivalry between what clinicians perceive as individuals from the same racial or immigrant group.

Many cultures highly value family loyalty and unselfishness. Consequently, speaking about being abused by a family member may go against what is of primary importance to immigrant women (Ho, 1990). Woman battering has been endorsed or neglected in many societies, which may make talking about it seem a danger in itself. "Bride burnings," which enable men to remarry and collect new dowries, occur in India's major cities on a daily basis (Stein, 1978). The Soviet government actively suppressed information about violence in the family until Perestroika in the late 1980s (Gondolf & Shestakov, in press).

The living circumstances of immigrant women also complicate their situation. They may be traditionally subjected to submissive roles as women and have greater dependency on their family members for economic survival. They are often likely to face religious taboos against leaving their relationships, and may also fear deportation or loss of assistance if they disclose abuse. Many women who would have turned to their extended family for support or help find themselves alone in the United States. They may not understand how to get money, live independently, or obtain social services and assistance from the police, and therefore need special help to survive as well as to find safety from battering (Sue & Sue, 1990).

As suggested in the discussion of Latina women, immigrant women in general often face complicated legal issues that restrict their access to services, employment, and new residences (Jang, 1994). Battering leaves them caught in a web of legal and economic issues that can be befuddling. A woman's immigration status may be jeopardized by attempting to leave or divorce her abusive partner. Not only could she be deported if she leaves her husband, she might lose the right to work. An immigrant woman may face complications in attempting to maintain custody of her children, and be especially vulnerable to having her children kidnapped by the batterer or his family members from his native country. Obtaining public assistance can also be more difficult or slowed by questions about immigration status.

The mere possibility of some of these problems, however remote, is often enough to constrain a woman from seeking help or exercising her rights. This is especially the case if the woman, as an immigrant, is not familiar with the nuances of the immigration laws or has been misinformed about her status by the batterer. The growing anti-immigration sentiment, moreover, helps reinforce a woman's doubts, hesitance, and fears.

Clinical Responses

Advocates recommend some additional steps to help immigrant women in general. One is for clinicians to pay particular attention to the terms and wording they use in asking about battering, abuse, and violence. Because of different perceptions and language differences, these terms may have to be carefully explained and illustrated. The effects of posttraumatic stress from civil war or strife also need special attention. Posttraumatic stress symptoms can easily be misinterpreted as resistance or denial of abuse. Conducting a broad social history may help expose abuses from persecution, repression, and war that might not otherwise surface in the presenting problems of an immigrant woman.

Advocates for immigrant women remind us not to confuse nonstandard English or dialects with a lack of intelligence or with personality traits. Immigrant women have usually demonstrated tremendous resourcefulness, ingenuity, and strength to be able to leave their native countries and gain entry into the United States. These qualities need to be identified, reinforced, and built on. The experiences of many immigrant women are likely to be so vastly different from most of our own that only someone directly familiar with their background may be able to get beyond appearances and tap the issues and potential they bring. Most of the manuals on cross-cultural counseling recommend having staff with diverse backgrounds, special cross-cultural expertise, and community linkages to help communicate with, interpret for, and advise immigrant women. Interpreters need to be educated about battering and understand confidentiality carefully or they might endanger immigrant women clients.

The second major step is to develop a more extensive outreach to immigrant women who are particularly vulnerable to language barriers, deportation threats, financial dependence, and family controls. Many immigrant women may be willing to endure woman battering in this country rather than return to oppression and violence in their native country. Paraprofessionals, community advocates, and outreach workers may be needed to help such women understand and accept the additional services they need and deserve. These workers may also be important in establishing the personal contact and rapport that is needed to build trust, increase disclosure, and interpret differences in meaning, experience, and perspective. Furthermore, they are likely to know where to get advice about a woman's immigration status and how to balance that with the woman's need to separate from a partner or simply seek help. Specialized immigrant and refugee programs may be essential in helping to obtain the additional support, resources, and services that so many immigrant women need to escape battering and establish safety.

■■ CONCLUSION

Battered women increasingly represent a diversity of racial, ethnic, and cultural backgrounds that warrants special attention. Although prevailing commonalities exist among battered women, important differences need to be considered in assessing woman battering. Advocates and cross-cultural manuals note the need to recognize differences in cultural attitudes, interaction, and expression that may be misinterpreted as personality traits or even mental disorders. They also point to social circumstances or living situations that may make it more difficult to obtain information about abuse and to enact safety plans or precautions.

Finally, these manuals make recommendations about the structure and organization of clinical practice. Clinicians may need to consult and collaborate with paraprofessionals, community workers, and advocates with cross-cultural experience and expertise to identify issues that need special attention. They might also benefit from being involved in community activities and efforts that expose them to a diversity of cultural values, issues, and circumstances. This sort of involvement can help in building rapport and interpreting information. It can also help in obtaining the additional support, assistance, and services that women of color and immigrant women need, but have difficulty obtaining because of discrimination, poverty, and mistrust.

7

Identifying and Assessing Men Who Batter

Assessment Issues

The challenge of identifying men who batter women is no less important than identifying battered women. Batterers present the source of abuse, fear, trauma, danger, and injury that has come to be known as woman battering. Identifying batterers in mental health services, however, has its own complications and pitfalls. The denial and manipulation of batterers can be beguiling. A man who has battered his female partner or wife may appear very rational, sane, and "together." If he does admit to abuse, he might seem regretful and contrite. He may be able to make his battering appear justified or momentary, or make it appear as part of his substance abuse or depression. Batterers, as a result, often elude identification in mental health settings, or clinicians minimize or neglect the battering that is reported or identified (Gondolf, 1990).

In this chapter, I raise fundamental issues that might help avoid some of the difficulties in assessing men who batter. The overall objective is to show how clinicians might contribute to the safety of battered women in the course of mental health assessments of men. I begin with a review of the specific questioning about assaultive behaviors that can help increase men's disclosing their woman battering and ways to confront the outright denial or manipulative admitting of battering. A discussion of issues involved with assessing the batterer is next. The use of profiles and typologies may be misleading, and attention to psychopathology may distract clinicians from the battering at hand. Finally, I pose several ways to help interrupt the battering and promote safety: avoidance strategies, cost-benefit analysis, and batterer program referral, as well as appropriate informing of the victim.

Many of the procedures and tools used to identify and assess battered women (see Chapter 4, "Procedures for Assessing Woman Battering") are applied here to men who batter—but with additional precautions. Confronting denial is more complicated and demanding with men in general (Hartman & Reynolds, 1987). Avoiding identification with, or sympathy for, men who admit battering is sometimes difficult because batterers are typically adept at manipulating and deceiving even professionals. Advocates and batterer counselors strongly encourage confronting men with the consequences of abuse, holding them accountable for their behavior, and taking steps to interrupt the battering (Pence & Paymar, 1993). In other words, it is not enough to ask routinely about abuse. The possibility of abuse needs to be probed and decisively addressed.

Safety Concerns

The fundamental concern of advocates is that women's safety is difficult to maintain within mental health services dealing with batterers (Adams, 1988; Hart, 1988; Pence, 1989). The focus on emotional states, psychological needs, and mental problems of the man as a client or patient can inadvertently leave the concerns and needs of the battered woman in the background. Diagnosis and treatment of mental disorders can unintentionally divert attention from the violence and what it takes to interrupt it and establish some semblance of safety. Additionally, many clinicians feel that confronting or reporting men's disclosure of woman battering disrupts the therapeutic relationship and treatment of mental problems (e.g., Stosny, 1995).

Research on a psychiatric emergency room shows how the report of violence is minimized or neglected (Gondolf, 1990). The majority of staff do not systematically inquire about violence, do not follow up men's mention of violence with specific questions, refer to the violence as a secondary or tangential problem, and/or do not offer referrals or intervention for the violence. Similarly, the majority of counselors who responded to a survey of marriage counselors do not prescribe steps to assess or address the battering suggested in case vignettes of woman battering (Hansen et al., 1981).

According to a study using the Domestic Violence Blame Scale, psychologists tend to blame the woman, as much as the man, for woman battering and focus on the "internal distribution" (e.g., alcohol abuse or emotional disorder) of the man and the woman (Petretic-Jackson & Jackson, 1996). The man's responsibility for his behavior appears to be diffused or deemphasized. Many of these oversights and tendencies are changing with increased personal awareness, academic education, and professional training about woman battering. At face value, however, they suggest that more needs to be done to improve the clinical response to men who batter women.

Battered women's advocates, along with many people working specifically with men who batter, are additionally concerned about the increased "psychologizing" of men who batter (Davis, 1987; Davis & Hagen, 1992). Many clinical psychologists are emphasizing the importance of identifying and treating the psychopathology of batterers (Geffner, 1995). The implicit assumption appears to be that psychopathology causes the violence, or at least seriously contributes to it. By treating the pathology, the violence will be reduced or ended. There is also the notion that different forms of pathology may warrant different forms of intervention and treatment. Consequently, men who have been arrested for woman battering or referred to batterer programs are increasingly being sent to mental health services for assessment, and mental health clinicians are being asked to consult with batterer programs or even serve as therapists in those programs.

■■ IDENTIFYING BATTERING

Denial and Minimization

Perhaps the greatest obstacle to the identification of woman battering among men is the tremendous denial, minimization, and justification associated with abuse. Numerous studies have documented the substantial discrepancy between what women report and what men report about

Minimizations	**Justification**
I'm here because the court sent me.	Things got out of control.
I only threatened her.	I just snapped.
I suppose she was afraid of me.	I just have a bad temper.
I sort of grabbed her.	I was drunk.
I only slapped her.	I was drunk.
I never really beat her up or anything.	She pushed my buttons.
She bruised easily.	She pushed too far.
We had a lovers' spat.	I was only defending myself.
Things just got a little heated.	What about her violence?
We had a little tussle.	She got hysterical on me.

Figure 7.1. Examples of Minimizations and Justifications
SOURCE: Pence & Paymar (1993).

battering incidents (Edleson & Syers, 1990; Jouriles & O'Leary, 1985; Riggs, Murphy, & O'Leary, 1989). In an evaluation study of arrested batterers in four cities, only a third (36%) of the men agreed with their partners' report that they had assaulted their partners sometime in the past; about a quarter (23%) agreed that the assault amounted to "severe violence," according to the categories of the Conflict Tactics Scale (Gondolf, 1996a). Comparison of self-reports to written arrest reports tend to confirm the women's reports, and suggest the arrest incident was more serious than even many women suggest.

A study of men in a substance abuse treatment unit further illustrates men's tendency to deny or minimize their battering. Approximately 40% of the men indicated on the Conflict Tactics Scale that they had physically assaulted their female partner in the previous year, whereas 80% of their partners reported being assaulted (Gondolf & Foster, 1991). Those men who did report an assault tended to report a less severe tactic (e.g., pushing instead of punching) and reported fewer tactics than their partners. In other words, the men minimized their battering by suggesting it was less severe and less extensive.

Batterer program manuals and guidebooks routinely discuss the tendencies of batterers to rationalize, justify, or excuse their abuse when they do admit to it (Gondolf, 1985; Kivel, 1992; Pence & Paymar, 1993; Russell, 1995; Stordeur & Stille, 1989). Batterers find fault or reason for the battering outside themselves (see Figure 7.1). They feel that they did what was necessary or right. The partner deserved what the batterer did—she asked for it. According to the man who batters his wife, the woman was "pushing his buttons," "backing him into a corner," or "making him mad." The man often perceives himself as retaliating for an emotional, verbal, or physical "assault" by the woman. Or she is violating, according to the man, some rule or expectation that he makes, judges, and enforces.

In the process, a batterer can make himself sound innocent and really believe he is so. In other cases, the man may not believe his claims, but becomes so familiar with conning and manipulating to "get his way" that he readily convinces himself and others that there is no problem. As O. J. Simpson reported to a sportscaster in 1989 after a documented arrest for battering Nicole, "It was not a big deal. Every couple has their lovers' spats." It becomes challenging for clinicians—and friends and family, for that matter—to separate a batterer's perceptions and deceptions from fact.

What appears as another extreme may be more of the same. As an in-depth study of incarcerated rapists concludes, men may appear not only as "deniers" but also as "admitters" (Scully & Marolla, 1984). Some men will readily admit their abuse and battering of women and, in the process, draw clinicians' sympathy and support. A batterer's admission may actually be manipulating others' sympathies to keep the focus on himself and make him look less culpable. As the rapist study points out, many of these men dismiss responsibility for their abuse similar to the "deniers." In admitting battering, they are saying that anger, drinking, stress, an abusive childhood, or a bad day made them do it. The cause or responsibility of the violence is projected outside of themselves. The violence, in the end, is minimized and diffused as another problem.

Confronting Denial

Inventory Questions

A great deal has been written about dealing with men's denial, withholding, projections, and manipulation in psychotherapy (e.g., Guillebeaux, Storm, & Demaris, 1986; Hartman & Reynolds, 1987; Meth & Pasick, 1990). The alcohol treatment field, for instance, identifies denial as a fundamental issue to confront. Getting individuals to realize that they have a problem, and to take responsibility for the problem, is a necessary step in changing behavior. It gives one what is sometimes referred to as *agency*. As long as the problem is "out there"—caused by somebody or something else—"I can't change it, because I have to change what is essentially beyond my control. I can, however, change myself and therefore can change problems that start with me"—or so the logic goes.

The techniques that have been used to help expose battering and prompt men to take responsibility are straightforward and commonplace. They are based on the notion of asking specific and direct questions about abuse and battering. A study of patients in a substance abuse treatment unit found that less than 5% of the clinical records indicate that any kind of domestic violence has been committed ever in the past, whereas nearly 40% of the men admit they assaulted their wives or partners in the past year (Gondolf & Foster, 1991). The question used for the clinical records was simply, "Have you ever been violent toward any of your family members?" as opposed to specific behavioral items on the Conflict Tactics Scale (Straus, 1979) used in the survey of the patients. The nature of the questions apparently made a difference in the amount of abuse and violence that was reported.

Rather than indirect or open-ended questioning frequently used in psychological evaluations, clinicians might routinely ask men about specific behaviors toward their partners. Men are more likely to admit to what appears as discrete behaviors, such as those drawn from any of the woman abuse inventories that ask specific questions (e.g., threw something, grabbed, pushed, shoved, slapped, hit). The separate admissions are likely to add up to a picture of abuse and battering.

As discussed in Chapter 4, "Procedures for Assessing Woman Battering," a woman battering inventory, such as the Index of Spouse Abuse (Hudson & McIntosh, 1981), might be administered in full to men. The total score can be used to confront the man, or separate items can be explored and elaborated. For instance, items about controlling or threatening one's partner might be discussed more fully, because these behaviors are often associated with physical abuse and battering. Simply breaking down and expanding a reported item or incident can expose other abusive behaviors.

- Describe what happened.
- What happened before that?
- What happened after that?
- What else did you want to do?
- What else did you do?

Funnel Questioning

Some batterer counselors recommend taking a gradual approach that approximates a kind of funnel questioning (Gondolf, 1985). The clinician might begin with general open-ended questions:

- How is your relationship going?
- What problems or tensions have you had recently?
- Tell me about any conflicts or hassles with your partner.
- Describe your arguments or disagreements—all couples have some.

The counselor then leads to specific questions about abusive behaviors.

- A lot of us get aggressive when we have conflicts or arguments. Have you ever thrown or hit something?
- Have you done any of the following toward your partner (ask about each behavior separately): grabbed, pushed, shoved, slapped, hit, punched, kicked, squeezed her neck, pulled her hair, used an object or weapon, forced her to have sex?

Admission to any of these behaviors should be followed with the usual questions about the use of other abusive tactics, the frequency and duration of the abuse, and the effect of the abuse on the perpetrator, the adult victim, and children.

A structured abuse inventory or funnel questioning basically uses the man's own piecemeal disclosures to incriminate him, so to speak. In the end, the clinician simply tells the man what the man told him: "It sounds to me like you have abused and battered your partner." The clinician has information from the man to back up the charge or identification of woman battering. Throughout the process, a clinician needs to be alert and even assertive. He or she must look for contradictions, cues, and hints of woman battering and promptly note them to the man and inquire about them.

Other Sources of Evidence

Clinicians can similarly use the "evidence" or information from other sources to identify woman battering and confront denial. A man may have been referred by the court, have an arrest record available, or have a civil protection order filed against him. Relatives or his partner may have reported information about the abuse to mental health staff, or the woman may have contacted a hospital or shelter suggesting that battering is a problem. Asking the man directly about actions his partner may have done may also indirectly expose the abuse. A clinician might ask the following questions.

- Has your partner ever threatened divorce or separation?
- Has your partner ever stayed overnight at a friend's because of your behavior?
- Has your partner ever contacted a shelter or women's program?
- Has your partner ever filed a protection order?
- Has your partner ever called the police about you?

Battered women's advocates and batterer counselors generally caution against soliciting and using information directly from a woman to confront a man's denial. Family and spousal confrontation has become popular in the alcohol treatment field as a way to break through denial about alcohol abuse. Using the woman's report either in a face-to-face meeting or indirectly through a clinician may jeopardize a woman's safety, however. A man could pressure, abuse, or batter his female partner in retaliation for disclosing information about him. He might attempt to limit her efforts to seek help or attempt to discredit her chances for child custody or financial assistance.

Evidence from the courts, police, or other agencies suggests that the problem is a social concern, that the community cares about it, and that sanctions are involved. This sort of "authority" is more likely not only to get a man's attention, but also to help shift the balance of power in his intimate relationship. It symbolically suggests that the community is on the woman's side; she is not isolated and defenseless.

Program Curriculum

Some batterer programs use a curriculum that systematically confronts men about their battering (Pence & Paymar, 1993). Each weekly session is devoted to defining, explaining, and illustrating a different aspect of abuse toward women. A program initially developed by the Domestic Abuse Intervention Program in Duluth, Minnesota, includes filmed vignettes and group exercises to demonstrate abusive behaviors and ways to avoid them. The list of abusive behaviors in Chapter 4, "Procedures for Assessing Woman Battering," illustrates the range of abusive behavior discussed:

- Intimidation through mean looks or smashing things
- Financial control by taking money or giving little cash to one's partner
- Coercion and threats by making a woman do illegal things or reporting her to welfare agencies
- Emotional abuse in the form of threats, put downs, and mind games
- Isolation through controlling what a woman does
- Using male privilege by making all the decisions and treating a woman like a servant

The theory is that these behaviors are highly associated with physical abuse and battering and together make up an abusive relationship of power and control. To address the physical abuse, one must address the larger constellation of controlling behaviors of which the battering is a part. Many men are simply not aware that many of their behaviors are abusive, because they have been taught much of their life that these are "normal" behaviors. As they are educated to see that much of their behavior toward their partner is abusive, they are more likely to admit their woman battering and accept responsibility for it.

Some detractors from a more therapeutic orientation argue that this approach of confronting, exposing, and identifying battering is too harsh (Stosny, 1995). Confronting battering, so the argument goes, puts men on the defensive, undercuts rapport necessary for a therapeutic relationship, and causes shame in clients who already have low self-esteem. Many women advocates and men's program staff, on the other hand, feel that confrontation can be done in a positive, supportive, and encouraging way. It helps to expose the problem, define it, and establish that it can be changed. Moreover, not identifying or neglecting the battering inadvertently condones and excuses it. This sort of oversight can reinforce the deception and manipulation that sustains many batterers. The stories of men who have continued woman battering because their behavior was not confronted in treatment fuels the concern about so-called compassionate approaches.

■■ ASSESSING PSYCHOPATHOLOGY

Batterer Profiles and Types

Profiles

Clinical assessments often rely on profiles to help identify individuals with certain kinds of problems or tendencies toward these problems. In fact, there is a tremendous push today for profiles, typologies, or indicators that might be used to identify risky or dangerous individuals. The problem is that a definitive profile or predictive typology of batterers has not as yet been established, and may not be possible (Gondolf & Hart, 1994). At the same time, clinicians need to be alert to the likelihood of more violence and take steps to interrupt it.

Preliminary studies of woman battering have proposed a batterer profile of an inexpressive, impulse-driven, traditional, and rigid personality with low self-esteem and frequent drug and alcohol problems (Dutton, 1988). Moreover, a recent set of studies of perhaps an atypical group of batterers seems to suggest the prevalence of a compulsive type of batterer with borderline personality tendencies. These men supposedly have attachment problems with women related to their abuse as young boys or domination by their mothers when they were young (Dutton, 1994; Dutton & Starzomski, 1993). This sort of profile, according to its proponents, suggests the need for therapy that addresses the men's victimization to reduce their violence. Less than 10% of a four-city sample of batterers (n = 840) appears to have such tendencies, however, according to the Million Clinical Multiaxial Inventory (MCMI). These men are not necessarily any less responsive to cognitive-behavioral or educational-oriented programs. In other words, the effort to typify batterers by psychological traits or tendencies does not appear to hold up across arrested batterers.

Much like the ongoing debate over the existence of an addictive personality in the alcohol field, the weight of evidence suggests that no conclusive batterer profile exists (Edleson, Eisikovits, & Guttman, 1985; Eisikovits & Edleson, 1989). Much of the profile is either based on limited clinical samples or contradicts itself. A comprehensive review of profile studies using comparison or control groups found that exposure to wife battering as a child, higher alcohol abuse, and lower socioeconomic status were the only consistent risk markers (Sugarman & Hotaling, 1989). Overall, the few studies with control groups suggest that, although batterers in treatment have more personality and alcohol problems than nonbatterers, batterers as a group do not substantially differ from the general population of men (Hamberger & Hastings, 1991).

Typologies

Empirical research on batterer characteristics has recently moved to the formulation of a typology of batterers (Holtzworth-Monroe & Stuart, 1994). One conception, based on batterers' behavior, suggests a continuum of sporadic, chronic, antisocial, and sociopathic batterers (Gondolf, 1988a). This typology is echoed in an additional study combining behavior indicators with several attitudinal scales. This later study found three similar batterer types: emotionally volatile, family-only, and generalized aggressors (Saunders, 1992b). A recent laboratory study (n=60) that observed the enactment of conflicts among couples found a physiological component that seemed to underlie two types (Gottman et al., 1995). One type appeared more "cold-hearted" in its abuse, registering a lower heart rate and less emotion. The other group was more "hot-blooded," showing higher heart rate and greater emotion.

Attempting to assess batterers clinically in terms of these types rather than a profile has its limitations. The typologies, developed through various post-hoc statistical procedures, are somewhat artificial. Few men may readily or obviously fit into the types. Each type includes a range of behaviors rather than the generalization that is usually used to describe them. It is also questionable how predictive the types are. We do not really know if a certain type of man will drop out of a program, reoffend, or be more dangerous. The effort to establish types of court-mandated batterers using behavioral indicators and psychological scores produced categories of antisocial versus more compulsive men; however, these types did not distinguish more severe violence at arrest (Gondolf, 1996b). The only indicator I could find associated with violence at arrest is the severity of past violence.

Dangerousness

Most advocates, nonetheless, encourage clinicians to examine the dangerousness and lethality of the batterer as part of their assessment.

Clinicians might use the same protocol for addressing dangerousness and lethality as is customarily used with battered women. The protocol, discussed in Chapter 4, includes inquiry about acute depression or delusions, threats and plans, obsessions and jealousy, stalking and kidnapping, and the use and availability of weapons (Hart, 1992). The problem is that these factors do not in themselves "predict" dangerousness or lethality, but they can give the clinician a fuller picture of the man and prompt the man toward greater self-examination and awareness (Gondolf & Hart, 1994).

Dangerousness assessments are further limited by the fact that batterers are generally the poorest source of information about their violence. As suggested above, they are typically prone to denial, distortion, and minimization. Without other sources of information (e.g., police records, partner testimony, hospital reports), a dangerousness assessment from the man may be misleading. The best source of information is usually a confidential interview with the woman, and any dangerousness assessment is primarily for her benefit. Therefore, the ideal may be to encourage the woman to contact a battered women's advocate and develop a dangerousness assessment and safety plan of her own.

Batterer Psychopathology

Mental health clinicians are usually charged with making some determination about men's psychological state in the form of a diagnosis about the clients they encounter. Clinical psychologists have recently pushed for the psychological assessment of batterers in general to propose appropriate treatment and expose the psychopathology that may be related to their abuse (American Psychological Association, 1996). Community surveys indicate that those with major disorders are more likely to be assaultive (Bland & Orn, 1986). Those with major depression and alcohol abuse tend to be the most violent.

According to our study of four batterer programs (n=840), approximately a quarter of court-mandated batterers may have major Axis I disorders and nearly half may have Axis II personality disorders, according to results of the MCMI (base rate scores of 85 or over; Gondolf, 1996a). As much as 90% of these batterers may have tendencies toward a clinical disorder of some kind (base rate scores of 75 or over; Gondolf, 1996a; Hamberger & Hastings, 1991). These studies indicate a variety of personality problems but no unified personality type, however (Hamberger

& Hastings, 1988). The personality inventories do not appear to distinguish batterers from other men with criminal problems, nor are they necessarily predictive of violence.

Our study of four batterer programs found no prevailing or distinguishing personality traits (Gondolf, 1996a). The subscale scores on the MCMI (base rate scores greater than 75) suggest that approximately one quarter of the men have narcissistic tendencies, another quarter have passive-aggressive tendencies, one fifth have depressive tendencies, and one fifth have antisocial tendencies. Over one third of the men (38%) scored high (base rate scores greater than 75) on four or more of the Axis II subscales. Our efforts to factor analyze these scores produced multiple combinations that did not conform to previous analysis of MCMI tests at other programs.

The research on psychiatric disorders among violent criminals in general suggests that psychopathology does not predict reoffense (Teplin, Abram, & McClelland, 1994).

Righteous Crime

Advocates propose that the vast majority of batterers, despite suggestions of different types, may be acting out of a similar mind-set. All the various manifestations or types of wife battering may be explained in terms of a belief system based on an egocentric perspective that holds one's needs and desires as primary (Gondolf, 1987). This belief system implies a moral order in which right and wrong are determined by one's own selfish interests and expectations. It is not that batterers are irrational or senseless. Their reasoning is often punishingly logical and value based. The problem is that their values are often distorted and their logic is self-serving. As Stoltenberg (1989) claims, wife battering is really an ethical issue, as opposed to a psychological or psychiatric one.

Interestingly, many criminologists attempting to revise the failed theories of deviance have pointed to a similar explanation for so-called crimes of passion. Even the most emotionally filled homicides may be related to a "righteous" belief system, according to criminologist Jack Katz (1988). Katz studied the accounts of those who had killed a family member in a crime of passion. He had not been directly involved in the domestic violence field, and he insists that he put aside theoretical biases to develop an explanation from the criminal's point of view. His relatively unbiased conclusion is that, whether the murder was highly planned or an explosive event, a righteous belief system was behind it. "These killers were defending both the morality of the social system and a personal claim of moral worth" (p. 19).

The perpetrators saw themselves as justified. They acted in response to what they saw to be a violation of their moral order—or some greater good. In many cases, being apprehended made the men feel like martyrs. This mind-set may account in part for why batterers often appear so logical on the surface, full of justifications, and "normal" in comparison to the victims they have devastated. The men do not see themselves at fault or as wrong. Instead, they project or attribute the blame to some external factors rather than to themselves (see Ptacek, 1988).

This mind-set also verifies why it is so important to confront denial, minimization, and excuses at the outset. They may be part of not only what sustains the battering but the cause itself. In some sense, the mind-set or belief system of batterers may be similar to the notion of "stinkin' thinkin'" of alcoholics. According to recent studies on masculinity and alcohol abuse, both alcohol abuse and men's violence may come from the same place in many men (Gondolf, 1995; Zubrestsky & Digirotama, 1996). They may both be ways to assert a sense of control, be manly, and feel a sense of power amid fear of intimacy, self-doubts, and insecurities.

The implication for clinicians is that psychopathology does not supersede the attention on battering. Woman battering needs to be identified and the underlying mind-set needs to be exposed. Although psychopathology of batterers may warrant special treatment, the treatment is unlikely to resolve or undo the violence itself. Moreover, men are likely to continue their abuse and battering during such treatment. Therefore, advocates urge clinicians to take steps that might at least help interrupt or contain a man's violence and steps that might help his female partner seek the support and assistance she may need.

■■ CLINICAL RESPONSE

Avoidance Strategies

Once clinicians identify woman battering and assess the batterer, the question remains what to do about it. The basic principles that advocates have proposed for responding to battered women apply to men who batter. The first is to develop what might be comparable to the safety plans for battered women, discussed in Chapter 4, "Procedures for Assessing Woman Battering." The second is to ensure referrals to specialized programs for woman battering, specifically batterer intervention and counseling programs. There is an additional and more delicate task of appropriately informing a battered woman of the assistance and support she might obtain. The objective overall is to interrupt the man's violence and promote the safety of the battered woman.

The first step of most batterer programs is to teach the men some techniques for avoiding violence (e.g., Gondolf & Russell, 1988). There are no illusions that these techniques can in themselves stop woman battering, and there is some concern that the techniques can be misused against a woman (Gondolf & Russell, 1986). With the proper precautions, these techniques can offer some men a temporary means for avoiding violence, at least until they become involved with the more extensive work of a batterer program. Many programs teach men how to take time-outs when they are feeling that they might become violent. Men with strong tendencies toward control are liable to use these time-outs as a quick fix or a crutch. They may use the time-outs as a way to cut off their partners or as a claim that they are cured—they know how to "handle" their problems now.

An alternative is to work with the man to develop his own strategies for avoiding abuse. This process is more likely to help him see the responsibility he has for stopping his abuse and to develop a procedure tailored to his situation. Avoidance strategies are usually based on the selective control that most batterers exercise: Most batterers hit their partners only at certain times and in certain places. They are also selective in that they do not usually treat or respond to others in the same way they do their female partners. Most have not, for instance, assaulted their bosses like they have their partners.

A set of reasons or "self-talk" often precedes the violence or predisposes the man to a violent act, according to cognitive theories of violence. A man might choose several actions following these thoughts. For some men, these thoughts and actions become somewhat habitual or automatic over time. The objective for a clinician, then, is to uncover what is sustaining the abusive habits or what sets the men in motion in the first place. The first questions a clinician might ask are:

Abuse is not worth it.	I don't have to get my way all the time.
Abuse is a crime.	Safety first.
There is no excuse for abuse.	She did not make me do it.
Blame is part of the problem.	The choice is mine.
Booze means more bruises.	I am not alone.
Control my behavior—not hers.	It's OK to ask for help.
Let go of my wife.	I can change.
Let it pass.	

Figure 7.2. Examples of Positive Self-Talk

- Why don't you hit others the way you've hit your partner when you are mad or offended by them?
- How do you avoid abusing or hitting them?

The clinician then might apply this line of questioning about the man's partner:

- Why have there been times when you wanted to hit your partner and you didn't?
- Why did you stop abusing her or not abuse her more severely?
- How have you avoided hitting her at times?
- How have you avoided battering her more severely at times when you were abusive?

The clinician might probe the responses to identify reasons and steps the man has successfully used to avoid violence. He or she might also suggest possibilities raised by other men to prompt more thought and to educate the man about further options. Some of the reasons for avoidance that often come up are "I knew I'd get into trouble, I felt it wasn't worth it," "Other people might see me," "I didn't want to hurt the kids." Some of the common options for avoidance are "I bit my tongue for the moment," "I walked away," "I called a friend on the phone," "I told my side of the story instead."

A list of reasons for not abusing and a list of steps he might take should be reviewed with the man and given to him for practice (see Figure 7.2). The clinician might, either at some follow-up time or in the course of the avoidance instruction, also identify reasons or steps that have backfired, such as going out to a bar or to a friend's house for a drink. The clinician might additionally discuss the implications or messages the proposed options might send to the man's partner. If he just "walks away," what is the woman likely to think and what is she likely to do—especially when the man returns? How might the man respond to these possibilities? The overall objective is to promote the use of positive thoughts and actions already familiar to the man and to further the process of applying these capabilities to potentially abusive situations.

Cost-Benefit Analysis

Clinicians might also conduct a kind of cost-benefit analysis with men identified as batterers. The object here is to help men weigh the consequences of their battering and, in the process, motivate them to seek and accept help. Advocates have argued that most batterers are highly egocentric, thinking primarily of their own needs and wants. Developmental and deterrence theories lend support to this assertion (Gelles, 1983; Gondolf, 1987). The implication is that clinicians need to appeal to a batterer's own self-interest to help interrupt violence and encourage him to change. A summary of the "costs" of being violent, as opposed to being nonviolent, can help a man see how the violence "hurts" him and why it is beneficial for him not to be violent. Conducting a cost-benefit analysis, as opposed to lecturing a man on why violence is wrong, also engages and involves a man who might be resistant or even defiant in his own self-assessment.

A cost-benefit analysis is relatively easy to conduct (see Figure 7.3). It is a matter of simply listing the costs, consequences, or problems associated with being violent, particularly toward one's partner. Then the clinician and man list the benefits, gains, or advantages he feels he gets from being violent. One might do the same cost-benefit listing for being nonviolent. As with the avoidance strategies, the clinician may need to suggest possibilities common to other men. He or she might raise some of the consequences often ignored or neutralized by men who batter. The clinician may need to extend especially the "consequences" side of the list because men on their own tend to pose more benefits than consequences. At the end of the exercise, the clinician might review the list with the man and ask him about the "bottom line" and what the

Benefits of Abuse	Costs of Abuse
1. I get my way.	1. My wife might leave me.
2. It shuts her up for a while.	2. She won't talk to me.
3. It releases tension.	3. I feel guilty afterward.
4. It keeps me from feeling hurt.	4. My kids pick up the violence.
5.	5. My kids are scared of me.
6.	6.
7.	7.
8.	8.
9.	9.
10.	10.

Benefits of Nonviolence	Costs of Nonviolence
1. It allows me to be myself.	1. I feel vulnerable.
2. I feel less ashamed.	2. I don't always get my way.
3. I experience intimacy.	3. I have to listen to criticism.
4. Our communication is better.	4. It takes more effort.
5.	5.
6.	6.
7.	7.
8.	8.
9.	9.
10.	10.

Figure 7.3. Weighing the Costs of Woman Abuse

cost-benefit analysis means for him. The bottom line should be that it is important for the man to get help and stick with that help.

Batterer Program Referral

The most appropriate form of help is batterer intervention or counseling programs. The programs generally involve a weekly group meeting of several hours that uses didactic and discussion methods to teach men to interrupt and avoid violence. Men should be involved in these specialized programs in addition to any individual counseling, substance abuse treatment, or mental health therapy in which they already participate to ensure that their abusive and battering behavior is system-

- A program duration of 6 to 12 months (some states accept a minimum of 4 months under certain situations)
- A protocol that systematically monitors and confronts abusive behavior
- Screening for alcohol and mental health problems with appropriate referrals or additional programming
- Identification of the range of controlling, abusive, and intimidating behaviors common to most batterers
- Instruction in avoidance techniques and responsibility plans
- Discussions and illustration of men's beliefs about power and control over women that underlie most men's battering
- Staff trained and experienced specifically in dealing with woman battering
- Linkages with battered women's programs and endorsement by them
- Coordination with courts, probation, and parole systems

Figure 7.4. Recommendations of State Standards for Batterer Programs

atically and regularly monitored, confronted, and addressed. As suggested above, other treatments tend not to attend to the violence directly or focus on safety issues.

The number and diversity of batterer programs have greatly increased in response to the domestic violence arrest laws established in the late 1980s (Gondolf, 1993). The programs have expanded to accommodate the increase in men being arrested and brought to court for battering their partners. Advocates have been working to bring quality control to the proliferation of batterer programs. They have attempted to draw on their experience with battered women to develop guidelines and standards that maximize safety for the women and minimize dangerous failures. Conclusive and sufficient "success rates" for batterer programs have not been established, but there is some indication that they at least contribute to a broader community effort to reduce woman battering (Eisikovits & Edleson, 1989; Gondolf, in press; Tolman & Bennett, 1990).

Batterer program standards, developed in at least 11 states, vary in specific details, but do suggest some common parameters that clinicians might consider in making referrals (see Figure 7.4). They set out recommendations for curriculum topics, program duration, program format, staff training, and relationships with other community services, police, and the courts. They encourage a tangible connection and collaboration with battered women's services to help ensure attention to the women's concerns (e.g., Hart, 1988; Pence, 1989). In fact, a local women's program is usually the best source for identifying batterer programs that meet such standards.

These standards note some program trends to be avoided (see also Adams, 1988):

• **Short-term anger management programs** focus on the men's emotional state and how to manage it. They teach techniques that identify provocation of the women, men's response to them, and alternatives to those responses. In the process, these programs often neglect the social reinforcements and deep-seated beliefs about battering that sustain many men's abuse. They also frequently give the illusion to men that they have been "cured" rather than encouraging long-term commitment to change.

• **In-depth psychodynamic programs** focus on the men's past trauma and current pains. This approach can inadvertently reinforce a man's egocentrism and justifications for his violence. It often takes the focus off the man's behavior toward his partner and the trauma, fear, and pain it is causing her—as opposed to him. Ideally, this sort of therapy might follow the long-term cognitive-behavior approach recommended in most state standards. The objective is to interrupt and avoid the violence first and then work on long-term personal issues that might contribute to reoffense. Most alcohol treatment programs similarly first conduct detoxification and sobriety before delving into issues associated with being a child of an alcoholic or suffering from chronic depression.

• **Couples counseling or couples groups,** following the popularity in marriage counseling, tend to focus on the interactions and communications between the man and the woman. Some such programs attempt to teach avoidance techniques jointly to the man and woman with the notion that the techniques work best if they are implemented by both partners. In the process, they may imply that the woman is an accomplice in the abuse and needs to take responsibility in ending it. The man, as a result, is likely to project and excuse his violence further, saying to himself, "It is her fault too." Women in couples groups, moreover, may be reluctant to report problems of abuse or face being punished by their partners if they do. Most practitioners consequently recommend that

- Call the National Hotline for Domestic Violence (1-800-799-7233), or the state toll-free hotline
- Call the local battered women's hotline
- Call the local victim service agency or legal aid program
- Call the local police for help
- Call a friend, relative, neighbor, or clergy
- Stay overnight at a friend's, relative's, or neighbor's house
- Join a support group for abused or battered women
- Go to a local battered women's shelter
- File for a protection for abuse in the civil court
- Press charges in a criminal court of law

Figure 7.5. Some Service and Safety Options for Women

couples counseling or couples groups be postponed until after a batterer program is complete and at least 6 to 9 months of nonviolence has been established (Edleson & Tolman, 1992).

Informing Battered Women

Options for the Woman

The most delicate response to identifying a man who batters is in contacting his battered partner or spouse. Most batterer programs suggest, at a minimum, informing the battered woman of the options for service, support, and protection (see Figure 7.5). Clinicians might also advise the woman about the limitations to psychotherapy and batterer counseling in stopping the abuse. This sort of information can help women in making decisions about their own safety and how best to respond to their situation. Some advocates recommend caution contacting the woman to assist in assessing the man or to report on his progress, however. The contact may put the woman at risk of reprisal or retaliation from her partner and encourage her to focus on him rather than get help for herself.

Clinicians might routinely advise the woman by phone, or in an individual session, about the importance of getting assistance for herself. She should know about the local battered women's program and the services it offers. She should be encouraged to contact it for further advice or in event of a crisis. Most of these centers maintain nonresidence support groups for women and referrals to other women's groups and individual therapists who specialize in helping battered women. They usually have programs for children who have witnessed violence as well. A woman should be informed about the importance of calling the police to help interrupt an incident and about the use of civil protection orders to remove a batterer temporarily from the home. Legal advocates are available through most battered women's programs to advise women about these options and assist them in enacting them.

Battered women generally have many misconceptions and false hopes about batterer counseling that need to be addressed. According to research on women in shelters, battered women are likely to return to their batterers who are in batterer programs, regardless of the severity of the men's battering and the extent of the women's resources (Gondolf, 1988b). Many women have been educated to view counseling as a panacea by friends and TV talk-shows or by their batterers themselves. Men frequently insist that by going to counseling they have been cured. The women may in response let down their guard or comply with the men's pressures and demands. Men, however, are most likely to obtain and stay in counseling if their partners have separated or if they have legal sanctions against them. Women also need to know that a referral or intake into a batterer program does not guarantee completion or safety. Between 30% and 60% of the men who enter batterer programs drop out in 3 months, and about 20% to 40% of the men who complete programs reoffend within 6 months to a year after the program (Gondolf, 1996b).

Contact Issues

Informing battered women may seem to some clinicians like an intrusion of the men's confidentiality or an opening to counseling the women along with the men. The confidentiality issue can usually be resolved by clarifying with a man at the outset that certain behaviors may require additional referral and notification for his and others' protection. Upon identifying battering, the clinician might add that he or she feels obligated ethically to notify the woman about seeking help, but that he or she will not break confidence about the specifics of anything the man has reported to him or her. The clinician might inquire about the man's response to this contact with the woman and use that response to assess the man further. If the man reacts defensively and defiantly, there is obviously grounds for elevated concern and perhaps required warning to the woman and maybe the police.

The "duty to warn" women or notify authorities is generally reserved for cases of imminent violence rather than cases of past severe violence. It is a matter of extrapolating from current behavior rather than predicting some future event that might occur (Sonkin, 1986). If a man is making threats, posing plans to harm, acting highly agitated, or clearly angry or enraged, then a clinician has a duty to warn a woman and urge her to take immediate action. She should contact friends and relatives, call a shelter, and notify the police. The clinician might also contact the police if violence appears imminent, especially if the woman cannot be reached or she is reluctant to take action on her own behalf. The clinician might again inform the man that he or she is ethically—and in some states legally—obligated to make such notification—and that it is ultimately in the man's interest that the clinician do so. Notifying the woman or police not only can help protect the woman, but also may keep the man from doing something that could land him in jail.

■■ CONCLUSION

Many battered women's advocates are cautious about counseling of any sort for men who batter. They feel that deterrent or punitive measures are the most appropriate given the criminal nature of woman battering, and the most effective, given the mind-set of most batterers. Most advocates have heightened concerns about the mental health assessments and treatment of men who batter. Mental health clinicians are sometimes inhibited by their nonjudgmental approach to counseling that may make them reluctant to confront the abuse and battering as clearly wrong. Their therapeutic focus may distract them from decisively attending to the violence and consistently working to interrupt it. The clinician's concern about confidentiality and rapport may also limit him or her from appropriately or sufficiently informing or warning women about men's violent tendencies.

To help improve the identification and assessment of batterers, clinicians are encouraged to apply much of the protocol proposed for battered women. They might use items from woman abuse inventories or administer an inventory in total. The inventory items might also be used as follow-up questions about the relationship in general. Questions about specific, concrete behavior appear to solicit more information than more open-ended and indirect questioning about abuse. Clinicians additionally might draw on other sources of evidence whenever possible to help challenge men's denial or verify their reports.

In assessing a man who batters, clinicians are cautioned about relying on profiles and typologies to distinguish batterers or predict their dangerousness. Conclusive diagnostic or predictive categories of batterers have yet to be established. Moreover, psychopathology does not appear to distinguish batterers or predict their dangerousness, and may distract from interrupting a man's tendency toward violence rooted in a mind-set of a "righteous crime." It is, of course, important to examine the dangerousness and lethality of the batterer in the form of current threats or plans of severe violence, obsession or jealousy about the partner, extreme depression or delusions, and ready use and fixation on weapons. Because much of this information is often difficult to obtain from the man, the best way to deal with dangerousness may be by having the woman contact a battered women's advocate about a risk assessment and safety plan.

Clinicians can take a few simple steps to help interrupt battering and contribute to the woman's safety. One is to promote some basic violence avoidance strategies that help a man think before he acts. A cost-benefit analysis that appeals to a man's self-interest can help a batterer identify the consequences of his battering and positive reasons to stop his battering. It may also encourage him to seek additional help. Clinicians might refer men who batter to specialized batterer programs that are often in a better position to confront men's denial and minimization of battering and systematically attend to the mind-set that sustains it. Advocates' advice on the quality and approach of batterer programs, however, needs to be considered in such referrals, because all batterer programs are not the same.

Finally, clinicians are encouraged to inform the battered woman about the options she has available to her. She needs to know about the social services and legal steps (calling the police, pressing charges, filing a protection order) that she can take in response to further abuse or battering. She also needs to know about the limitations of psychotherapy and batterer counseling in stopping violence and the importance of taking care of herself and her children. Clinicians also should establish a means to warn women in the event they detect imminent violence or threat of violence.

In sum, clinicians have a special challenge in assessing men who come to them for help. They need to identify woman battering by systematically and routinely asking hard questions in the face of denial and minimization. They need to move beyond conventional profiles, typologies, or psychiatric diagnoses to assess violence. They are encouraged to go beyond the usual boundaries of their work to inform battered women of their options and risks. In this way, they are more likely to contribute not only to the well-being of the man as a client or patient but also to the safety and survival of the battered woman.

 **Appendix**

A Survey of Battered Women's Advocates

with Susan Schechter, MSW

There have been many speculations about what needs to be done to improve the response of mental health services to women battering. Some advocates point to the need for woman battering training or assessment tools and procedures. Others raise broader concerns about the differences in assumptions, organization, and practices of mental health services that ultimately need to be addressed to accommodate battered women. At the same time, numerous developments suggest cooperation between advocacy for battered women and mental health treatment. There have been joint trainings on women battering and mental health, study groups on diagnosis and assessment, and treatment manuals for therapists.

A survey of advocacy programs for battered women suggests that battered women's programs predominately deal with the criminal justice system (Edleson, 1993). They assist in obtaining protection orders from the civil courts, help with the prosecution of batterers, and assist women in divorce or custody cases. In the process, advocates have contact with district attorneys and prosecutors, private attorneys and legal aid services, magistrates and judges, and probation and parole officers. Also, many advocates provide training for police, criminal justice officials, and other agencies and organizations and do policy work around interventions, funding, and services for battered women.

From a national listing of battered women's programs, researchers randomly surveyed 379 advocacy programs in the United States (Edleson, 1993). Three fourths of the programs reported working with other agencies and systems on behalf of battered women. Only a third reported working with health and mental health services. This result may reflect the fact that the vast majority (87%) of advocacy programs offer counseling and emotional support along with information, referrals, and representation for battered women. Many battered women's advocates may consequently feel that battered women's services offer sufficient "treatment" for most battered women, or may feel that the mental health services are not beneficial to many battered women.

Increased collaboration with mental health services may be shown to improve the well-being and safety of battered women. Battered women's programs tend to offer primarily short-term crisis-oriented services. Many women are likely to benefit from services that extend beyond the scope of these programs. Also, related research implies that mental health services coupled with advocacy are likely to be more effective and beneficial. For instance, studies of the coordination of battered women programs and the criminal justice system indicate improved and more effective intervention on behalf of battered women (Gamache, Edleson, & Schock, 1988; Steinman, 1988). Battered women advocates have helped bring about increased arrests, convictions, and court mandated counseling of batterers.

To assess the relationship of battered women's programs and mental health services better, the National Resource Center on Domestic Violence conducted a survey of state domestic violence coalitions in the spring of 1994. A mailed survey was developed to estimate the extent of existing cooperation between battered women's programs and mental health services, problems and barriers to cooperation and innovations and possibilities for collaboration. The survey represents the perspective of battered women's advocates and should be complemented by future surveys of mental health professionals. The experience of those specializing in working with and for battered women offers an important first step in developing a strategy to improve mental health services' response to battered women, however. Battered women's advocates have a direct involvement in the issues facing battered women, and have observed the problems that battered women encounter in obtaining and receiving mental health services.

■■ METHODOLOGY

The survey was conducted through a mailed questionnaire to the 50 state coalitions for domestic violence. These coalitions represent and coordinate the battered women's programs in their respective states. To varying extents, they offer technical assistance, staff training, program development, legal advice, and state funding to local shelters. They also initiate policy recommendations and legislative action to their respective state governments. State coalitions vary in size and sophistication. The majority of the state coalitions have between two and five staff members, and several coalitions have been operating for 15 years or more. Pennsylvania and Texas coalitions have over 20 staff members working on a variety of state projects, and additionally house national projects such as the National Resource Center on Domestic Violence and the National Domestic Violence Hotline. Approximately 10 states have less than two staff members coordinating communication among their state battered women's programs and between state legislatures and the women's programs. As of 1994, all the state coalitions received funding from the U.S. Department of Health and Human Services to maintain operations and coordinate provisions of the Violence Against Women Act.

Coalitions not responding to the mailed questionnaire within a month were contacted by phone and asked to submit the completed survey to the National Resource Center on Domestic Violence. Thirty state coalitions returned completed surveys reporting for 896 battered women's programs. The number of completed surveys represents a response rate of 60% of the existing state coalitions. The 20 state coalitions not responding to the survey were compared to the responding coalitions in terms of size, number of shelters, and model programming.[1] The nonrespondents were not dissimilar on any of these criteria, suggesting that the responding sample may be fairly representative of the states as a whole. Approximately one quarter of the completed surveys were based on the state coalitions polling the battered women's programs in their states, and the rest were estimates made by state coalition staff reflecting their experience working with their state's programs. The average number of programs per state was 31, ranging from a few in Hawaii to 106 in New York.

The survey was developed by one policy and one research consult-ant to the National Resource Center on Domestic Violence, based on preliminary discussions and interviews with approximately 10 national, state, and local advocates. The three-page questionnaire mailed to the state coalitions consisted of two main parts. The first part included three inventories of practices between battered women's programs and men-tal health services. The inventories listed practices initiated or received by battered women's programs during the previous 2 years. The second part comprised seven open-ended questions inquiring about major bar-riers or problems, collaborative innovations and improvements, state guidelines or standards, training materials, needed tools or materials, and recommended actions for the National Resource Center.

The responses for the two inventories about the relationship of battered women's programs and mental health services were tabulated as follows: The total number of women's programs that had done or received certain practices was divided by the total number of women's programs represented by the responding state coalitions (Tables 2.1 and 2.2). The inventory for training materials currently in use was analyzed using the percentage of state coalitions indicating "yes" for each item. The open-ended questions were categorizations of the responses listed by each state coalition (Table 2.3). The percentages in Tables 2.1, 2.2, and 2.3 are the number of states with a response corresponding to that particular category divided by the total number of states responding to that question. All the reporting state coalitions responded to the open-ended question asking about major barriers to cooperation between battered women's programs and mental health services (Table 1.1); only one half to three quarters of the states offered answers to the other open-ended questions about training materials used, needed tools or materials, existing innovations, and recommendations for the National Resource Center.

◼◼ CONCLUSION

The survey of state coalitions of battered women's programs produced several instructive findings presented in Part I of this book. A majority of the women's programs already have a relationship with mental health services through mutual referrals, consultation, and training. A substantial portion of state coalitions report significant obstacles to furthering these relationships or developing new ones where none currently exit, however. The barriers include inappropriate mental health treatment, mental health clinicians' lack of understanding about women battering, mental health clinicians' lack of respect for battered women's advocates, and costly and inaccessible services. The survey respondents call for more training information and materials to help address these barriers and share more of advocates' expertise with mental health clinicians. A variety of innovations to bring together battered women's advocates and mental health clinicians are already underway and hold promise for further collaborations. More needs to be done to advance these emerging efforts and to establish a coordinated national initiative, however. According to the respondents, a national organization such as the National Resource Center on Domestic Violence might help compile and refine training materials, build linkages with mental health professional organizations, and develop criteria for referrals, agency assessment, and certifications.

Despite these apparent trends, the survey also revealed a great range of concerns and practices. The differences from state to state and from one community to another were striking. Battered women's programs in some states have developed elaborate cooperative relationships with mental health services and are eager to advance these relationships. In other communities, there is great distrust and little interest in collaboration, often because of the philosophical and professional differences mentioned in Chapter 1. Moreover, some disagreement exists among advocates themselves on how best to proceed on many important issues, especially when and where to refer battered women with mental health problems. The support of training and referral among the coalitions and their respective programs is, nonetheless, very clear. A need remains for more refined and developed materials, materials for a variety of audiences (including graduate students), and a compilation of assessment protocols.

The efforts and prospects of collaboration pose new questions and issues that might best be resolved through further collaboration. One place to start is with some of the basics that this book attempts to compile. The one resounding theme throughout the survey is that for collaboration to increase, mental health clinicians need to be better apprised of the expertise of battered women's advocates. They need to be made aware of the nature of woman battering and its effects, and they need to be more informed about the difficult safety issues that face battered women and the complications that mental health diagnoses and treatment bring to many battered women. They need to be informed of the services that battered women's programs can offer and the work the programs do.

This agenda is obviously one-sided, because many battered women's advocates feel as if their expertise has been neglected by many mental health clinicians. The survey suggests, too, that many women's services are eager for the professional assistance of mental health clinicians as possible referral sources, consultants, board members, and intervention colleagues. The ultimate goal is for a communitywide response to women battering that offers women the comprehensive assistance they need and deserve. The survey suggests that advocates see that happening in collaboration with mental health clinicians.

▟ NOTE

1. The states not responding were California, Colorado, Delaware, Florida, Idaho, Iowa, Kentucky, Louisiana, Maryland, Massachusetts, Minnesota, Mississippi, Montana, New Mexico, North Carolina, Oregon, South Dakota, Washington, Wisconsin, and Wyoming.

Recommended Bibliography

■■ OVERVIEWS

American Psychological Association (1996). *Violence and the family: Report of the American Psychological Association Presidential Task Force on Violence and the Family.* Washington, DC: American Psychological Association.

Browne, A. (1993). Violence against women by male partners: Prevalence, outcomes, and policy implications. *American Psychologist, 48,* 1077-1087.

Gondolf, E. (1990). *Psychiatric response to family violence.* Lexington, MA: Lexington Books.

Gondolf, E. W., & Fisher, E. R. (1991). Wife battering. In R. Ammerman & M. Hersen (Eds.), *Case studies in family violence.* New York: Plenum.

Jordan, C., & Walker, R. (1994). Guidelines for handling domestic violence cases in community mental health clinics. *Hospital and Community Psychiatry, 45,* 147-151.

Koss, M., Goodman, L., Browne, A., Fitzgerald, L., Keita, G. P., & Russo, N. F. (1994). *No safe haven: Male violence against women at home, at work, and in the community.* Washington, DC: American Psychological Association.

Saunders, D. (1992). Woman battering. In R. Ammerman & M. Hersen (Eds.), *Assessment of family violence: A clinical and legal sourcebook.* New York: John Wiley.

Schechter, S. (1987). *Guidelines for mental health practitioners in domestic violence cases.* Washington, DC: National Coalition Against Domestic Violence.

Schechter, S. (1994). *Survey of battered women state coalitions on mental health services.* Harrisburg, PA: National Resource Center on Domestic Violence.

Warshaw, C. (1993). Domestic violence: Challenges to medical practice. *Journal of Women's Health, 2,* 73-80.

Warshaw, C. (1995). *Violence and women's health: Old models, new challenges.* In Center for Mental Health Services, *Dare to vision: Shaping the national agenda for women, abuse, and mental health services* (pp. 67-85). Holyoke, MA: Human Resource Association.

Worell, J., & Remer, P. (1992). *Feminist perspectives in therapy: An empowerment model for women.* New York: John Wiley.

■■ BATTERING ASSESSMENT INSTRUMENTS

Girder, L. (1990). Mediation triage: Screening for spouse abuse in divorce mediation. *Mediation Quarterly, 7,* 365-376.

Hudson, W., & McIntosh, S. (1981). The assessment of spouse abuse: Two quantifiable dimensions. *Journal of Marriage and the Family, 43,* 873-884.

Marshall, L. (1992). Development of the Severity of Violence Against Women Scales. *Journal of Family Violence, 7,* 103-121.

Rodenburg, F., & Fantuzzo, J. (1993). The measure of wife abuse: Steps toward the development of a comprehensive technique. *Journal of Family Violence, 8,* 203-227.

Sanders, D., Lynch, A., Grayson, M., & Linz, D. (1987). The inventory of beliefs about wife beating: The construction and initial validation of a measure of beliefs and attitudes. *Violence and Victims, 2,* 39-57.

Schwartz, M., & Mattley, C. (1993). The Battered Woman scale and gender identities. *Journal of Family Violence, 8,* 277-287.

Shepard, M., & Campbell, J. (1992). The abusive behavior inventory: A measure of psychological and physical abuse. *Journal of Interpersonal Violence, 7,* 291-305.

Smith, P. H., Earp, J. A., & DeVellis, R. (1995). *Measuring battering: Development of the Women's Experience with Battering (WEB) Scale.* Presented at the Fourth International Family Violence Conference, Durham, NH, July 24.

Straus, M. (1979). Measuring intrafamily conflict and violence: The Conflict Tactics (CT) Scales. *Journal of Marriage and the Family, 41,* 75-88.

Tolman, R. (1989). The development of a measure of psychological maltreatment of women by their male partners. *Violence and Victims, 4,* 159-177.

■■ RELATED ASSESSMENT INSTRUMENTS

Briere, J., & Runtz, M. (1989). The trauma symptom checklist (TSC-33): Early data on a new scale. *Journal of Interpersonal Violence, 4,* 151-163. (Effects of childhood sexual abuse on adults).

Horwitz, M., Wilner, N., & Alvarez, W. (1979). Impact of Event Scale: A measure of subjective stress. *Psychosomatic Medicine, 41,* 209-218.

Keane, T., Malloy, P., & Fairbank, J. (1984). Empirical development of an MMPI subscale for the assessment of combat related post-traumatic stress disorder. *Journal of Consulting and Clinical Psychology, 52,* 888-891.

Morrison, E. (1988). Instrumentation issues in the measurement of violence in psychiatric inpatients. *Issues in Mental Health Nursing, 9,* 9-16.

Ruch, L., Gartrell, J., Amedeo, S., & Coyne, B. (1991). The sexual assault symptom scale: Measuring self-reported sexual assault trauma in the emergency room. *Psychological Assessment, 3,* 3-8.

Saunders, B. E., Kilpatrick, D. G., & Resnick H. S. (1989). Brief screening for lifetime history of criminal victimization at mental health intake: A preliminary study. *Journal of Interpersonal Violence, 4,* 267-758.

Watson, C. (1990). Psychometric post-traumatic stress disorder measurement techniques: A review. *Psychological Assessment, 2,* 460-469.

▪▪ LETHALITY AND DANGEROUSNESS

Campbell, J. C. (1986). Nursing assessment of risk on homicide with battered women. *Advances in Nursing Science, 8,* 36-51.

Gondolf, E. W., & Hart, B. (1994). Lethality and dangerousness assessments. *Violence Update, 4,* 7-10.

Hart, B. (1990). Assessing whether batterers will kill. *Ending Men's Violence Network Newsletter, 8,* 16.

Saunders, D. G. (1994). Prediction of wife assault. In J. Campbell (Ed.), *Assessing the risk of dangerousness: Potential for further violence of sexual offenders, batters, and child abusers.* Thousand Oaks, CA: Sage.

Sherman, L., Schmidt, J., Rogan, D., & DeRiso, C. (1991). Predicting domestic homicide: Prior police contact and gun threats. In M. Steinman (Ed.), *Woman battering: Policy responses.* Cincinnati, OH: Anderson.

Teplin, L., Abram, K., & McClelland, G. (1994). Does psychiatric disorder predict violent crime among released jail detainees? A six-year longitudinal study. *American Psychologist, 49,* 335-347.

▪▪ DIAGNOSIS AND TREATMENT

Bograd, M. (1984). Family systems approaches to wife battering: A feminist critique. *American Journal of Orthopsychiatry, 54,* 558-568.

Brown, L. S. (1992). A feminist critique of personality disorders. In L. S. Brown & M. Ballou (Eds.), *Personality and psychopathology: Feminist reappraisals.* New York: Guilford.

Dutton, M. A. (1992). *Empowering and healing the battered woman: A model for assessment and intervention.* New York: Springer.

Janoff-Bulman, R., & Frieze, I. (1983). A theoretical perspective for understanding reactions to victimization. *Journal of Social Issues, 39,* 1-17.

Rieker, P., & Carmen, E. (1984). *The gender gap in psychotherapy: Social realities and psychological processes.* New York: Plenum.

Rieker, P. P., & Carmen, E. H. (1986). The victim-to-patient process: The disconfirmation and transformation of abuse. *American Journal of Orthopsychiatry, 56,* 360-370.

Schellenback C., Trickett, P., & Susman, E. (1991). A multimethod approach to the assessment of physical abuse. *Violence and Victims, 6,* 57-73.

Veltkamp, L., & Miller, T. (1990). Clinical strategies in recognizing spouse abuse. *Psychiatric Quarterly, 61,* 179-187.

Walker, L. E. A. (1989). Psychology and violence against women. *American Psychologist, 44,* 695-702.

Walker, L. E. A. (1994). *Abused women and survivor therapy.* Washington, DC: American Psychological Association.

■■ POSTTRAUMATIC STRESS DISORDER

Astin, M., Lawrence, K., & Foy, D. (1993). Posttraumatic stress disorder among battered women: Risk and resiliency factors. *Violence and Victims, 8,* 17-28.

Campbell, J. C. (1990). Battered woman syndrome: A critical review. *Violence Update, 1*(4), 1, 4, 10.

Campbell, J. C. (1993). Post-traumatic stress in battered women: Does the diagnosis fit? *Issues in Mental Health Nursing, 14,* 173-186.

Douglas, M. A. (1987). The battered woman syndrome. In D. J. Sonkin (Ed.), *Domestic violence on trial.* New York: Springer.

Dutton, M. A. (1992). Assessment and treatment of PTSD among battered women. In D. Foy (Ed.), *Treating PTSD: Procedure for combat veterans, battered women, adult and child sexual assaults.* New York: Guilford.

Herman, J. L. (1992). *Trauma and recovery.* New York: Basic Books.

Janoff-Bulman, R. (1992). *Shattered assumptions: Toward a new psychology of trauma.* New York: Free Press.

Kemp, A., Rawlings, E. I., & Green, B. L. (1991). Post-traumatic stress disorder in women: Diagnosis and treatment of battered woman syndrome. *Psychotherapy, 28,* 21-34.

■■ ASSESSMENT RESEARCH

Gondolf, E. W. (1992). Discussion of violence in psychiatric evaluations. *Journal of Interpersonal Violence, 7,* 334-349.

Jacobson, A. (1989). Physical and sexual assault histories among psychiatric outpatients. *American Journal of Psychiatry, 146,* 755-758.

Jacobson, A., Koehler, J., & Jones-Brown, C. (1987). The failure of routine assessment to detect histories of assault experienced by psychiatric patients. *Hospital and Community Psychiatry, 38,* 396-389.

Jacobson, A., & Richardson, B. (1987). Assault experiences of 100 psychiatric inpatients: Evidence of the need for routine inquiry. *American Journal of Psychiatry, 144,* 908-913.

Kurz, D. (1987). Emergency department responses to battered women: Resistance to medicalization. *Social Problems, 34,* 69-81.

McFarlane, J., Parker, B., Soeken, K., & Bullock. L. (1992). Assessing for abuse during pregnancy. *Journal of the American Medical Association, 267,* 3176-3178.

McLeer, S. V., & Anwar, R. (1989). A study of battered women presenting in an emergency department. *American Journal of Public Health, 79,* 65-76.

McLeer, S. V., Anwar, R., Herman, S., & Maquiling, K. (1989). Education is not enough: A systems failure in protecting battered women. *Annals of Emergency Medicine, 18,* 651-653.

Rose, K., & Saunders, D. G. (1986). Nurses' and physicians' attitudes about women abuse: The effects of gender and professional role. *Health Care for Women International, 7,* 427-438.

Stark, E., Flitcraft, A., & Frazier, W. (1979). Medicine and patriarchal violence: The social construction of a "private" event. *International Journal of Health Services, 9,* 461-493.

Sugg, N. K., & Inui, T. (1992). Primary care physician's response to domestic violence: Opening Pandora's box. *Journal of the American Medical Association, 267,* 3157-3178.

Warshaw, C. (1989). Limitations of the medical model in the care of battered women. *Gender & Society, 3,* 506-517.

▟ IMPACT RESEARCH

Aguilar, R. J., & Nightingale, N. N. (1994). The impact of specific battering experiences on self-esteem of abused women. *Journal of Family Violence, 9,* 35-46.

Astin, M. C., Lawrence, K. J., & Foy, D. W. (1993). Posttraumatic stress disorder among battered women: Risk and resiliency factors. *Violence and Victims, 8,* 53-68.

Foy, D., Sipprelle, R., Rueger, D., & Carroll, E. (1984). Etiology of posttraumatic stress disorder in Vietnam veterans: Analysis of premilitary, military, and combat exposure influences. *Journal of Consulting and Clinical Psychology, 52,* 79-87.

Gleason, W. J. (1993). Mental disorders in battered women: An empirical study. *Violence and Victims, 8,* 29-40.

Gondolf, E. W., & Fisher, E. R. (1988). *Battered women as survivors: An alternative to treating learned helplessness.* Lexington, MA: Lexington Books.

Graham, D., Rawlings, E., & Rimini, N. (1988). Survivors of terror: Battered women, hostages, and the Stockholm Syndrome. In K. Yllö & M. Bograd (Eds.), *Feminist perspectives on wife abuse.* Newbury Park, CA: Sage.

Hamilton, J. A. (1989). Emotional consequences of victimization and discrimination in special populations of women. *Psychiatric Clinicians of North America, 12,* 35-51.

Horwitz, M. J., Wilner, N. U., & Alvarez, W. (1979). Impact of event scale: A measure of subjective stress. *Psychosomatic Medicine, 41,* 209-218.

Housekamp, B. M., & Foy, D. W. (1991). The assessment of posttraumatic stress disorder in battered women. *Journal of Interpersonal Violence, 6,* 367-375.

Rosewater, L. B. (1988). Battered or schizophrenic? Psychological tests can't tell. In K. Yllö & M. Bograd (Eds.), *Feminist perspectives on wife abuse.* Newbury Park, CA: Sage.

Walker, L. E. A. (1984). *The battered woman syndrome.* New York: Springer.

▟ MEDICAL SOCIOLOGY

Anspach, R. R. (1988). Notes on the sociology of medical discourse: The language of case presentation. *Journal of Health and Social Behavior, 29,* 357-375.

Fisher, S. (1986). *In the patient's best interest: Women and the politics of medical decisions.* New Brunswick, NJ: Rutgers University Press.

Kuipers, J. C. (1989). Medical discourse in anthropological context: Views of language and power. *Medical Anthropology Quarterly, 3,* 99-123.

Mishler, E. (1981). Viewpoint: Critical perspectives on the biomedical model. In E. Misheler (Ed.), *Social contexts of health, illness and patient care.* Cambridge, MA: Harvard University Press.

Mishler, E. (1984). *The discourse of medicine: Dialectics of medical interviews.* Norwood, NJ: Ablex.

Russell, L. (1994). *Educated guesses: Making policy about medical screening tests.* Berkeley: University of California Press.

Waitzkin, H. (1984). Doctor-patient communication: Clinical implications of social scientific research. *Journal of the American Medical Association, 252,* 2441-2446.

Waitzkin, H. (1985). Information giving in medical care. *Journal of Health and Social Behavior, 26,* 81-101.

Waitzkin, H. (1989). A critical theory of medical discourse: Ideology, social control, and the processing of social context in medical encounters. *Journal of Health and Social Behavior, 30,* 220-239.

■■ BATTERER ISSUES

Dutton, D. G., & Starzomski, A. (1993). Borderline personality in perpetrators of psychological and physical abuse. *Violence and Victims, 8,* 327-339.

Edleson, J. L., & Tolman, R. M. (1992). *Intervention for men who batter: An ecological approach.*
Newbury Park, CA: Sage.

Gondolf, E. W. (1988). Who are those guys? Towards a behavioral typology of men who
batter. *Violence and Victims, 3,* 187-203.

Gondolf, E. W. (1993). Male batterers. In R. Hampton (Ed.), *Family violence: Prevention and
treatment.* Newbury Park, CA: Sage.

Gondolf, E. W., & Foster, R. A. (1992). Wife assault among V.A. alcohol rehabilitation
patients. *Hospital and Community Psychiatry 40,* 74-79.

Hamberger, L. K., & Hastings, J. E. (1988). Characteristics of male spouse abusers consistent
with personality disorders. *Hospital and Community Psychiatry, 39,* 763-770.

Pence, E., & Paymar, M. (1993). *Education groups for men who batter: The Duluth model.* New
York: Springer.

Saunders, D. G. (1992). A typology of men who batter: Three types derived from cluster
analysis. *American Journal of Orthopsychiatry, 62,* 264-275.

Sonkin, D. J. (1987). The assessment of court-mandated male batterers. In D. J. Sonkin
(Ed.), *Domestic violence on trial.* New York, Springer.

Sugarman, D., & Hotaling, G. (1989). Violent men in intimate relationships: An analysis
of risk markers. *Journal of Applied Social Psychology, 19,* 1034-1048.

■■ GUIDES FOR BATTERED WOMEN

Ackerman, R., & Pickering, S. (1995). *Before it's too late: Helping women in controlling or
abusive relationships.* Deerfield Beach, FL: Health Communications. (A guidebook
especially for men in abusive relationships where there are also drug or alcohol
problems.)

Bowker, L. (1986). *Ending the violence: A guidebook based on the experiences of one thousand
battered wives.* Holmes Beach, FL: Learning Publications. (Personal and formal
strategies that have helped end woman abuse.)

Gondolf, E. (1989). *Man against woman: What every woman should know about violent men.*
Blue Ridge Summit, PA: TAB/McGraw Hill. (A frank discussion of the reasons for
men's violence and the prospects for changing.)

Jones, A., & Schechter, S. (1992). *When love goes wrong: Strategies for women with controlling
partners.* New York: HarperCollins. (An analysis of abuse as a means of control and
degradation that includes practical advice and methods for obtaining safety and
change.)

NiCarthy, G. (1986). *Getting free: A handbook for women in abusive relationships.* Seattle, WA:
Seal. (One of the most popular guides for women on dealing with abuse.)

References

Ackerman, R. J. (1987). *Different houses, different homes: Why adult children of alcoholics are not the same*. Deerfield, FL: Health Communications.

Adams, D. (1988). Treatment models of men who batter: A pro-feminist analysis. In K. Ylló & M. Bograd (Eds.), *Feminist perspectives on wife abuse*. Newbury Park, CA: Sage.

Allen, P. (1990). Violence and the American Indian woman. In *The speaking profits us: Violence in the lives of women of color*. Seattle: SAFECO.

American Psychiatric Association (1994). *Diagnostic and statistical manual of mental disorders* (4th ed.). Washington, DC: Author.

American Psychological Association (1996). *Violence and the family: Report of the American Psychological Association Presidential Task Force on Violence and the Family*. Washington, DC: Author.

Amoja Three Rivers. (1990). Cultural etiquette: A guide for the well-intentioned. Indian Valley, VA: Market Vimmin.

Anspach, R. R. (1988). Notes on the sociology of medical discourse: The language of case presentation. *Journal of Health and Social Behavior, 29,* 357-375.

Appelbaum, P. S. (1988). The new preventive detention: Psychiatry's problematic responsibility for the control of violence. *American Journal of Psychiatry, 145,* 779-785.

Arias, I., & Beach, S. (1987). Validity of self-reports of marital violence. *Journal of Family Violence, 2,* 139-149.

Astin, M. C., Lawrence, K. J., & Foy, D. W. (1993). Posttraumatic stress disorder among battered women: Risk and resiliency factors. *Violence and Victims, 8,* 53-68.

Bell, C. (1991). Clinical care update: Preventive strategies for dealing with violence among blacks. In R. Hampton (Ed.), *Black family violence: Current research and theory*. Newbury Park, CA: Sage.

Binder, R. L., & McNiel, D. (1986). Victims and families of violent psychiatric patients. *Bulletin of American Academic Psychiatry Law, 14,* 131-139.

Bland, R., & Orn, H. (1986). Family violence and psychiatric disorder. *Canadian Journal of Psychiatry, 31,* 129-137.

Bograd, M. (1984). Family systems approaches to wife battering: A feminist critique. *American Journal of Orthopsychiatry, 54,* 558-568.

Bograd, M. (1992). Values in conflict: Challenges to family therapists' thinking. *Journal of Marital and Family Therapy, 18,* 245-256.

Bonilla-Santiago, G. (1996). Latina battered women: Barriers to service delivery and cultural considerations. In A. Roberts (Ed.), *Helping battered women: New perspectives and remedies.* New York: Oxford University Press.

Bowker, L. (1983). *Beating wife beating.* Lexington, MA: Lexington Books.

Bowker, L. (1993). A battered woman's problems are social, not psychological. In R. Gelles & D. Loseke (Eds.), *Current controversies on family violence.* Newbury Park, CA: Sage.

Bowker, L. (1995). *Adapting the battered women syndrome to criminal justice evidentiary conventions.* Presented at the fourth international Family Violence Research Conference, Durham, NH, July 21-24.

Brown, L. S. (1992). A feminist critique of personality disorders. In L. S. Brown & M. Ballou (Eds.), *Personality and psychopathology: Feminist reappraisals.* New York: Guilford.

Browne, A. (1987). *When battered women kill.* New York: Free Press.

Browne, A. (1993). Violence against women by male partners: Prevalence, outcomes, and policy implications. *American Psychologist, 48,* 1077-1087.

Browne, A. (1995a). Building new lives from a model of strength. In Center for Mental Health Services, *Dare to vision: Shaping the national agenda for women, abuse and mental health services.* Holyoke, MA: Human Resources Association.

Browne, A. (1995b). *Violence, poverty, and minority status in the lives of women and children: Implications for violence prevention.* Keynote address at the National Violence Prevention Conference, Des Moines, IA, October 23.

Campbell, D., Campbell, J., King, C., Parker, B., & Ryan, J. (1994). The reliability and factor structure of the Index of Spouse Abuse with African-American Women. *Violence and Victims, 9,* 259-274.

Campbell, J. C. (1986). Nursing assessment of risk on homicide with battered women. *Advances in Nursing Science, 8,* 36-51.

Campbell, J. C. (1990). Battered woman syndrome: A critical review. *Violence Update, 1(4),* 1,4,10.

Campbell, J. C. (1993). Post-traumatic stress in battered women: Does the diagnosis fit? *Issues in Mental Health Nursing, 14,* 173-186.

Campbell, J. C. (1995). *Depression in battered women.* Paper presented at the fourth international Family Violence Research Conference, Durham, NH, July 21-24.

Campbell, R., Sullivan, C., & Davidson, W. (1995). Women who use domestic violence shelters: Changes in depression over time. *Psychology of Women Quarterly, 19,* 237-255.

Caplan, G. (1964). *Principles of preventive psychiatry.* New York: Basic.

Caplan, P. (1985). *The myth of female masochism.* New York: Dutton.

Carmen, E. (1995). Victim-to-patient-to-survivor processes: Clinical perspectives. In Center for Mental Health Services, *Dare to vision: Shaping the national agenda for women, abuse, and mental health services.* Holyoke, MA.

Carmen, E., Rieker, P., & Mills, T. (1984). Victims of violence and psychiatric illness. *American Journal of Psychiatry, 141,* 378-383.

Carver, C. S., Scheier, M. F., & Weintraub, J. K. (1989). Assessing coping strategies: A theoretically based approach. *Journal of Personality and Social Psychology, 56,* 267-283.

Cascardi, M., & O'Leary, K. D. (1992). Depressive symptomatology, self-esteem, and self-blame in battered women. *Journal of Family Violence, 7,* 249-259.

Cazenave, N., & Straus, M. (1979). Race, class network embeddedness and family violence: A search for potent support systems. *Journal of Comparative Family Studies, 10,* 281-299.

Center for Mental Health Services. (1995). *Dare to vision: Shaping the national agenda for women, abuse and mental health services.* Holyoke, MA: Human Resources Association.

Chamberlin, J. (1978). *On our own: Patient-controlled alternatives to the mental health system.* Lawrence, MA: National Empowerment Center.

Chesler, P. (1972). *Women and madness.* Garden City, NJ: Doubleday.

Chester, B., Robin, R., Koss, M., Lopez, J., & Goldman, D. (1994). Grandmother dishonored: Violence against women by male partners in American Indian communities. *Violence and Victims, 9,* 259-274.

Chu, J., & Dill, D. (1990). Dissociative symptoms in relation to childhood psychological and sexual abuse. *American Journal of Psychiatry, 147,* 887-892.

Coley, S., & Beckett, J. (1988). Black battered women: Practice issues. *Social Casework, 69,* 483-490.

Conrad, P., & Schneider, J. (1985). *Deviance and medicalization: From badness to sickness.* Columbus, OH: Merrill.

Cowger, C. (1994). Assessing client strengths: Clinical assessment for client empowerment. *Social Work, 39,* 262-268.

Crenshaw, K. (1994). Mapping the margins: Intersectionality, identity politics, and violence against women of color. In M. S. Fineman (Ed.), *The public nature of private violence.* New York: Routledge.

Davis, L. V. (1987). Battered women: The transformation of a social problem. *Social Work, 32,* 306-311.

Davis, L. V., & Hagen, J. (1992). The problem of wife abuse: The interrelationship of social policy and social work practice. *Social Work, 37,* 15-20.

Deegan, P. (1995). Before we dare to vision, we must be willing to see. In Center for Mental Health Services, *Dare to vision: Shaping the national agenda for women, abuse and mental health services.* Holyoke, MA: Human Resources Association.

Denzin, N. K. (1987). *Treating alcoholism: An Alcoholics Anonymous approach.* Newbury Park, CA: Sage.

Dobash, R. E., & Dobash, R. P. (1992). *Women, violence and social change.* New York: Routledge.

Douglas, M. A. (1987). The battered woman syndrome. In D. J. Sonkin (Ed.), *Domestic violence on trial.* New York: Springer.

Dunham, H. W. (1976). *Social realities and community psychiatry.* New York: Human Sciences.

Dutton, D. G. (1988). Profiling of wife assaulters: Preliminary evidence for a trimodal analysis. *Violence and Victims, 3,* 5-30.

Dutton, D. G. (1994). Behavioral and affective correlates of borderline personality organization in wife assaulters. *International Journal of Law and Psychiatry, 17,* 265-277.

Dutton, D. G., & Starzomski, A. (1993). Borderline personality in perpetrators of psychological and physical abuse. *Violence and Victims, 8,* 327-337.

Dutton, M. A. (1992a). Assessment and treatment of PTSD among battered women. In D. Foy (Ed.), *Treating PTSD: Procedure for combat veterans, battered women, adult and child sexual assaults.* New York: Guilford.

Dutton, M. A. (1992b). *Empowering and healing the battered woman: A model for assessment and intervention.* New York: Springer.

Dutton, M. A., Perrin, S., & Chrestman, K. (1995). *Differences among battered women's MMPI profiles: The role of context.* Paper presented at the fourth international Family Violence Research Conference, Durham, NH, July 21-24.

Edleson, J. (1993). Advocacy services for battered women. *Violence Update, 4*(4), 1-2, 4, 10.

Edleson, J. L., Eisikovits, Z. C., & Guttman, E. (1985). Men who batter women: A critical review of the evidence. *Journal of Family Issues, 6,* 229-247.

Edleson, J., & Syers, M. (1990). Gender differences in reporting of battering incidences. *Family Relations, 35,* 377-382.

Edleson, J. L., & Tolman, R. M. (1992). *Intervention for men who batter: An ecological approach.* Newbury Park, CA: Sage.

Eisikovits, Z. C., & Edleson, J. L. (1989). Intervening with men who batter: A critical review of the literature. *Social Service Review, 37,* 385-414.

Ferraro, K., & Johnson, J. (1983). How women experience battering: The process of victimization. *Social Problems, 30,* 325-339.

Fisher, S. (1986). *In the patient's best interest: Women and the politics of medical decisions.* New Brunswick, NJ: Rutgers University Press.

Flaskerud, J. (1986). The effects of culture-compatible intervention on the utilization of mental health services by minority clients. *Community Mental Health Journal, 22,* 127-141.

Fossum, M. (1989). *Catching fire: Men coming alive in recovery.* New York: Harper & Row.

Foster, R., & Gondolf, E. W. (1989). From social worker to batterer counselor. *Response, 12,* 3-5.

Frank, P., & Kadison, G. (1992). Blaming by naming: Battered women and the epidemic of codependence. *Social Work, 37,* 5-6.

Frankl, V. (1959). *Man's search for meaning: An introduction to logotherapy.* Boston: Beacon.

Gamache, D., Edleson, J., & Schock, M. (1988). Coordinated police, judicial and social service response to woman battering: A multi-baseline evaluation across three communities. In G. Hotaling, D. Finkelhor, J. Kirkpatrick, & M. Straus (Eds.), *Coping with family violence: Research and policy perspectives.* Newbury Park, CA: Sage.

Geffner, R. (1995). Of mice, humans, and family violence. *Family Violence and Sexual Assault Bulletin, 11*(3-4), 3-4.

Gelles, R. (1983). An exchange/social control theory. In D. Finkelhor, R. Gelles, G. Hotaling, & M. Straus (Eds.), *The dark side of families: Current family violence research.* Beverly Hills, CA: Sage.

Girder, L. (1990). Mediation triage: Screening for spouse abuse in divorce mediation. *Mediation Quarterly, 7,* 365-376.

Gleason, W. J. (1993). Mental disorders in battered women: An empirical study. *Violence and Victims, 8,* 29-40.

Goldstein, J. (1990). Strength or pathology: Ethical and rhetorical contrasts in approaches to practice. *Families in Society, 71,* 267-275.

Gondolf, E. W. (1983). Institution/neighborhood interface: A case study of divergent perspectives. *Journal of the Community Development Society, 14,* 73-92.

Gondolf, E. W. (1985). *Men who batter: An integrated approach to stopping wife abuse.* Holmes Beach, FL: Learning Publications.

Gondolf, E. W. (1987). Changing men who batter: A developmental model of integrated interventions. *Journal of Family Violence, 2,* 345-369.

Gondolf, E. W. (1988a). Who are those guys? Towards a behavioral typology of men who batter. *Violence and Victims, 3,* 187-203.

Gondolf, E. W. (1988b). The effect of batterer counseling on shelter outcome. *Journal of Interpersonal Violence, 3,* 275-289.

Gondolf, E. W. (1990). *Psychiatric response to family violence.* Lexington, MA: Lexington Books.

Gondolf, E. W. (1992). Discussion of violence in psychiatric evaluations. *Journal of Interpersonal Violence, 7,* 334-349.

Gondolf, E. W. (1993). Male batterers. In R. Hampton (Ed.), *Family violence: Prevention and treatment.* Newbury Park, CA: Sage.

Gondolf, E. W. (1995). Alcohol abuse, wife assault, and power needs. *Social Service Review, 69,* 274-284.

Gondolf, E. W. (1996a). *Characteristics of batterers in a multi-site evaluation of batterer intervention systems.* Report to the Centers for Disease Control and Prevention (CDC), Atlanta, GA.

Gondolf, E. W. (1996b). *Characteristics of battered women whose batterers are in court-mandated counseling.* Report to the Centers for Disease Control and Prevention (CDC), Atlanta, GA.

Gondolf, E. W. (in press). Batterer programs: What we know and need to know. *Journal of Interpersonal Violence.*

Gondolf, E. W., & Fisher, E. R. (1988). *Battered women as survivors: An alternative to treating learned helplessness.* Lexington, MA: Lexington Books.

Gondolf, E. W., Fisher, E. R., & McFerron, R. (1991). Racial differences among shelter residents: A comparison of Anglo, black, and Hispanic battered women. In R. Hampton (Ed.), *Black family violence: Current research and theory.* Newbury Park, CA: Sage.

Gondolf, E. W., & Foster, R. (1991). Wife assault among V.A. alcohol rehabilitation patients. *Hospital and Community Psychiatry, 42,* 74-79.

Gondolf, E. W., & Hart, B. (1994). Lethality and dangerousness assessments. *Violence Update, 4,* 7-10.

Gondolf, E. W., & Russell, D. (1986). The case against anger control for batterers. *Response, 9*(3), 2-5.

Gondolf, E. W., & Russell, D. (1988). *Man to man: A guide to men in abusive relationships.* New York: Sulzburger & Graham.

Gondolf, E. W., & Shestakov, D. (in press). Spousal homicide in Russia: Gender inequality in a multi-factor model. *Violence Against Women.*

Gordon-Bradshaw, R. H. (1988). A social essay on special issues facing poor women of color. *Women and Health, 12,* 243-259.

Gottman, J., Jacobson, N., Rushe, R., Short, J., Babcock, J., La Taillade, J., & Waltz, J. (1995). The relationship between heart rate, reactivity, emotionally aggressive behavior and general violence in batterers. *Journal of Family Psychology, 9,* 1-41.

Guillebeaux, F., Storm, C., & Demaris, A. (1986). Luring the reluctant male: A study of males participating in marriage and family therapy. *Family Therapy, 13,* 216-225.

Hamberger, L. K., & Hastings, J. E. (1988). Characteristics of male spouse abusers consistent with personality disorders. *Hospital and Community Psychiatry, 39,* 763-770.

Hamberger, L. K., & Hastings, J. E. (1991). Personality correlates of men who batter and nonviolent men: Some continuities and discontinuities. *Journal of Family Violence, 6,* 131-148.

Hammer, M., & Stanton, S. (1993). *Reengineering the corporation.* New York: HarperCollins.

Hansen, J., Harway, M., & Cervantes, N. (1981). Therapists' perceptions of severity in cases of family violence. *Violence and Victims, 6,* 225-235.

Hansen, M. (1993). Feminism and family therapy: A review of feminist critiques of approaches to family violence. In M. Hansen & M. Harway (Eds.), *Battering and family therapy: A feminist perspective.* Newbury Park, CA: Sage.

Hart, B. (1988). *Safety for women: Monitoring batterers programs*. Harrisburg, PA: Pennsylvania Coalition Against Domestic Violence.

Hart, B. (1992). Assessing whether batterers will kill. *Ending Men's Violence Network Newsletter, 8,* 16.

Hart, B., & Stuehling, J. (1992). *Personalized safety plan*. Reading, PA: Pennsylvania Coalition Against Domestic Violence.

Hartman, C., & Reynolds, D. (1987). Resistant clients: Confrontation, interpretation, and alliance. *Social Casework, 68,* 205-213.

Hawkins, D. (1987). Devalued lives and racial stereotypes: Ideological barriers to the prevention of family violence among blacks. In R. Hampton (Ed.), *Violence in the black family: Correlates and consequences*. Lexington, MA: Lexington Books.

Herman, J. L. (1992). *Trauma and recovery*. New York: Basic Books.

Ho, C. K. (1990). An analysis of domestic violence in Asian-American communities: A multi-cultural approach to counseling. In L. Brown & M. Root (Eds.), *Diversity and complexity in feminist therapy*. New York: Haworth.

Holtzworth-Munroe, A. (1988). Causal attributions in marital violence: Theoretical and methodological issues. *Clinical Psychological Review, 8,* 331-334.

Holtzworth-Munroe, A., & Stuart, R. (1994). Typologies of male batterers: Three subtypes and the differences among them. *Psychological Bulletin, 116,* 476-497.

Horwitz, M., Wilner, N., & Alvarez, W. (1979). Impact of Event Scale: A measure of subjective stress. *Psychosomatic Medicine, 41,* 209-218.

Housekamp, B. M., & Foy, D. W. (1991). The assessment of posttraumatic stress disorder in battered women. *Journal of Interpersonal Violence, 6,* 367-375.

Hudson, W., & McIntosh, S. (1981). The assessment of spouse abuse: Two quantifiable dimensions. *Journal of Marriage and the Family, 43,* 873-884.

Huisman, K. (1996). Wife battering in Asian American communities: Identifying the service needs of an overlooked segment of the U.S. population. *Violence Against Women, 2,* 102-118.

Jacobson, A. (1989). Physical and sexual assault histories among psychiatric outpatients. *American Journal of Psychiatry, 146,* 755-758.

Jacobson, A., Koehler, J., & Jones-Brown, C. (1987). The failure of routine assessment to detect histories of assault experienced by psychiatric patients. *Hospital and Community Psychiatry, 38,* 396-389.

Jacobson, A., & Richardson, B. (1987). Assault experiences of 100 psychiatric inpatients: Evidence of the need for routine inquiry. *American Journal of Psychiatry, 144,* 908-913.

Jang, D. (1994). Caught in a web: Immigrant women and domestic violence. *National Clearinghouse for Legal Services Review, Special Issue,* 397-405.

Janoff-Bulman, R. (1992). *Shattered assumptions: Toward a new psychology of trauma*. New York: Free Press.

Jones, A., & Schechter, S. (1992). *When love goes wrong: Strategies for women with controlling partners*. New York: HarperCollins.

Jouriles, E. N., & O'Leary, K. D. (1985). Interpersonal reliability of reports of marital violence. *Journal of Consulting and Clinical Psychology, 53,* 419-421.

Kantor, G., Jasinski, J., & Aldarondo, E. (1994). Sociocultural status and incidence of marital violence in Hispanic families. *Violence and Victims, 9,* 207-222.

Kasl, C. (1992). *Many roads, one journey: Moving beyond the twelve steps*. San Francisco: Harper & Row.

Katz, J. (1988). *Seductions of crime: Moral and sensual attractions in doing evil*. New York: Basic Books.

Kaufman, G. (1992). The mysterious disappearance of battered women in family therapists' offices. *Journal of Marital and Family Therapy, 18,* 233-244.

Keane, T., Malloy, P., & Fairbank, J. (1984). Empirical development of an MMPI subscale for the assessment of combat related post-traumatic stress disorder. *Journal of Consulting and Clinical Psychology, 52,* 888-891.

Kemp, A., Rawlings, E. I., & Green, B. L. (1991). Post-traumatic stress disorder in women: Diagnosis and treatment of battered woman syndrome. *Psychotherapy, 28,* 21-34.

Kivel, P. (1992). *Men's work: How to stop the violence that tears our lives apart.* Center City, MN: Hazelden.

Koss, M., Goodman, L., Browne, A., Fitzgerald, L., Keita, G. P., & Russo, N. F. (1994). *No safe haven: Male violence against women at home, at work, and in the community.* Washington, DC: American Psychological Association.

Kuipers, J. C. (1989). Medical discourse in anthropological context: Views of language and power. *Medical Anthropology Quarterly, 3,* 99-123.

Kurz, D. (1987). Emergency department responses to battered women: Resistance to medicalization. *Social Problems, 34,* 69-81.

Lidz, C., & Mulvey, E. (1990). Institutional factors affecting psychiatric admission and commitment decisions. In G. Weisz (Ed.), *Social science perspectives on medical ethics.* New York: Kluwer Academic Publishers.

Lifton, R. (1968). *Death in life: Survivors of Hiroshima.* New York: Random House.

Loseke, D. (1992). *The battered women and shelters: The social construction of wife abuse.* Albany: State University of New York Press.

Lum, D. (1992). *Social work practice and people of color: A process-stage approach.* Pacific Grove, CA: Brooks/Cole.

Mahoney, M. (1991). Legal images of battered women: Redefining the issue of separation. *Michigan Law Review, 90,* 1-94.

Marín, G., & Marín, B. (1991). *Research with Hispanic populations.* Newbury Park, CA: Sage.

Marshall, L. (1992). Development of the Severity of Violence Against Women Scales. *Journal of Family Violence, 7,* 103-121.

McFarlane, J., Parker, B., Soeken, K., & Bullock. L. (1992). Assessing for abuse during pregnancy. *Journal of the American Medical Association, 267,* 3176-3178.

McLeer, S. V., & Anwar, R. (1989). A study of battered women presenting in an emergency department. *American Journal of Public Health, 79,* 65-66.

McLeer, S. V., Anwar, R., Herman, S., & Maquiling, K. (1989). Education is not enough: A systems failure in protecting battered women. *Annals of Emergency Medicine, 18,* 651-653.

McLellan, A. T., Luborsky, L., Cacciola, J., Griffith, J., McGahan, P., & O'Brien, C. (1985). *Guide to the Addiction Severity Index, background, administration, and filed testing results.* Rockville, MD: U.S. Department of Health and Human Services.

Meth, R., & Pasick, R. (1990). *Men in therapy: The challenge of change.* New York: Guilford.

Mills, T. (1985). The assault on the self: Stages in coping with battering husbands. *Qualitative Sociology, 8,* 103-123.

Mishler, E. (1984). *The discourse of medicine: Dialectics of medical interviews.* Norwood, NJ: Ablex.

Mitchell, R., & Hodson, C. (1983). Coping with domestic violence: Social support and psychological health among battered women. *American Journal of Community Psychology, 11,* 629-654.

Moore, S. (1994). Battered woman syndrome: Selling the shadow to support the substance. *Howard University Law Review, 38,* 297-352.

Morrison, E. (1988). Instrumentation issues in the measurement of violence in psychiatric inpatients. *Issues in Mental Health Nursing, 9*, 9-16.

Mulvey, E., & Lidz, C. (1993). Measuring patient violence in dangerousness research. *Law and Human Behavior, 17*, 277-288.

Neff, J., Holamon, B., & Schluter, T. D. (1995). Spousal violence among Anglos, blacks and Mexican Americans: The role of demographic variables, psychosocial predictors, and alcohol consumption. *Journal of Family Violence, 10*, 1-21.

Neighbors, H. (1984). Professional help use among black Americans: Implications for unmet need. *American Journal of Community Psychology, 12*, 551-566.

Nowotny, M. L. (1989). Assessment of hope in patients with cancer: Development of an instrument. *Oncology Nursing Forum, 16*(5), 7-61.

O'Carroll, P., & Mercy, J. (1986). Patterns and recent trends in black homicide. In D. Hawkins (Ed.), *Homicide among black Americans.* Lanham, MD: University Press of America.

Peck, M. S. (1978). *The road less traveled: A new psychology of love, traditional values, and spiritual growth.* New York: Simon & Schuster.

Peck, M. S. (1987). *The different drum: Community-making and peace.* New York: Simon & Schuster.

Pence, E. (1989). Batterer programs: Shifting from community collusion to community confrontation. In P. L. Caesar & L. K. Hamberger (Eds.), *Treating men who batter: Theory, practice, and programs.* New York: Springer.

Pence, E., & Paymar, M. (1993). *Education groups for men who batter: The Duluth model.* New York: Springer.

Perilla, J., Bakerman, R., & Norris, R. (1994). Culture and domestic violence: The ecology of abused Latinas. *Violence and Victims, 9*, 325-339.

Petretic-Jackson, P., & Jackson, T. (1996). Mental health interventions with battered women. In A. Roberts (Ed.), *Helping battered women: New perspectives and remedies.* New York: Oxford University Press.

Ponterotto, J., Casas, J. M., Suzuki, L., & Alexander, C. (1995). *Handbook of multicultural counseling.* Thousand Oaks, CA: Sage.

Powers, M. (Ed.). (1988). *Oglala women: Myth, ritual, and reality.* Chicago: University of Chicago Press.

Proctor, E., & Davis, L. (1994). The challenge of racial difference: Skills for clinical practice. *Social Work, 37*, 314-321.

Ptacek, J. (1988). Why do men batter their wives? In K. Yllö & M. Bograd (Eds.), *Feminist perspectives on wife abuse.* Newbury Park, CA: Sage.

Rappaport, J. (1977). *Community psychology: Values, research, and action.* New York: Holt, Rinehart & Winston.

Richie, B. (1996). *Compelled to crime: The gender entrapment of battered black women.* New York: Routledge.

Rieker, P., & Carmen, E. (1984). *The gender gap in psychotherapy: Social realities and psychological processes.* New York: Plenum.

Rieker, P, & Carmen, E. (1986). The victim-to-patient process: The disconfirmation and transformation of abuse. *American Journal of Orthopsychiatry, 56*, 360-370.

Riggs, D. S., Murphy, C. M., & O'Leary, K. D. (1989). Intentional falsification in reports of interpartner aggression. *Journal of Interpersonal Violence, 4*, 220-232.

Rose, K., & Saunders, D. G. (1986). Nurses' and physicians' attitudes about women abuse: The effects of gender and professional role. *Health Care for Women International, 7*, 427-438.

Russell, L. (1994). *Educated guesses: Making policy about medical screening tests.* Berkeley: University of California Press.

Russell, M. N. (1995). *Confronting abusive beliefs: Group treatment for abusive men.* Thousand Oaks, CA: Sage.

Saleeby, D. (Ed.). (1992). *The strengths perspective in social work practice: Power in the people.* Plains, NY: Longman.

Santiago, A., & Morash, M. (1994). Strategies for serving Latina battered women. In J. Garber & R. Turner (Eds.), *Gender in urban research.* Thousand Oaks, CA: Sage.

Saunders, B. E., Kilpatrick, D. G., & Resnick H. S. (1989). Brief screening for lifetime history of criminal victimization at mental health intake: A preliminary study. *Journal of Interpersonal Violence, 4,* 267-758.

Saunders, D. (1988). Wife abuse, husband abuse, or mutual combat. In K. Yllö & M. Bograd (Eds.), *Feminist perspectives on wife abuse.* Newbury Park, CA: Sage.

Saunders, D. (1992a). Woman battering. In R. Ammerman & M. Hersen (Eds.), *Assessment of family violence: A clinical and legal sourcebook.* New York: John Wiley.

Saunders, D. (1992b). A typology of men who batter: Three types derived from cluster analysis. *American Journal of Orthopsychiatry, 62,* 264-275.

Saunders, D. (1994). Prediction of wife assault. In J. Campbell (Ed.), *Assessing the risk of dangerousness: Potential for further violence of sexual offenders, batters, and child abusers.* Newbury Park, CA: Sage.

Schechter, S. (1982). *Women and male violence: The visions and struggles of the battered women's movement.* Boston: South End.

Schechter, S. (1987). *Guidelines for mental health practitioners in domestic violence cases.* Washington, DC: National Coalition Against Domestic Violence.

Schechter, S. (1994). *Survey of battered women state coalitions on mental health services.* Harrisburg, PA: National Resource Center on Domestic Violence.

Scheff, T. J., & Culver, D. M. (1964). Ascriptive elements in the psychiatric screening of mental patients in a midwestern state. *Social Problems, 11,* 401-413.

Scheier, M. F., & Carver, C. S. (1985). Optimism, coping, and health: Assessment and implications of generalized outcome expectancies. *Health Psychology, 4,* 219-247.

Scully, D., & Marolla, J. (1984). Convicted rapists' vocabulary of motive: Excuses and justifications. *Social Problems, 31,* 530-544.

Segal, S. P., Watson, M. A., Goldfinger, S. M., & Averbuck, D. S. (1988). Civil commitment in the psychiatric emergency room. *Archives of General Psychiatry, 45,* 748-763.

Shea, S. C. (1988). *Psychiatric interviewing: The art of understanding.* Philadelphia: W.B. Saunders.

Shepard, M., & Campbell, J. (1992). The Abusive Behavior Inventory: A measure of psychological and physical abuse. *Journal of Interpersonal Violence, 7,* 291-305.

Sherman, L., Schmidt, J., Rogan, D., & DeRiso, C. (1991). Predicting domestic homicide: Prior police contact and gun threats. In M. Steinman (Ed.), *Woman battering: Policy responses.* Cincinnati, OH: Anderson.

Shupe, A., Stacey, W., & Hazelwood, L. (1987). *Violent men, violent couples: The dynamics of domestic violence.* Lexington, MA: Lexington Books.

Simon, B. (1990). Rethinking empowerment. *Journal of Progressive Human Services, 1,* 27-40.

Sonkin, D. (1986). Clairvoyance versus commonsense: Therapists' duty to warn and protect. *Violence and Victims, 1,* 7-21.

Sorenson, S., & Telles, C. (1991). Self-reports of spousal violence in a Mexican-American and Non-Hispanic white population. *Violence and Victims, 6,* 3-15.

Stark, E., & Flitcraft, A. (1988). Violence among intimates: An epidemiological review. In V. Van Hasselt, R. Morrison, A. Bellack, & M. Hersen (Eds.), *Handbook of family violence*. New York: Plenum.

Stark, E., & Flitcraft, A. (1996). *Women at risk: Domestic violence and women's health.* Thousand Oaks, CA: Sage.

Stefan, S. (1995). The protection racket—Violence against women: Psychiatric labeling and the law. In Center for Mental Health Services, *Dare to vision: Shaping the national agenda for women, abuse and mental health services*. Holyoke, MA: Human Resources Association.

Stein, D. (1978). Women to burn: Suttee as a normative institution. *Signs, 4,* 253-273.

Steinman, M. (1988). Evaluating a system-wide response to domestic violence: Some initial findings. *Journal of Contemporary Criminal Justice, 4,* 172-186.

Stoltenberg, J. (1989). *Refusing to be a man: Essays on sex and justice*. New York: Meridian.

Stordeur, R. A., & Stille, R. (1989). *Ending men's violence against their partners: One road to peace*. Newbury Park, CA: Sage.

Stosny, S. (1995). *Treating attachment abuse: A compassionate approach*. New York: Springer.

Straus, M. (1979). Measuring intrafamily conflict and violence: The Conflict Tactics (CT) Scales. *Journal of Marriage and the Family, 41,* 75-78.

Straus, M. (1990). The Conflict Tactics Scales and its critics: An evaluation and new data on validity and reliability. In M. Straus & R. Gelles (Eds.), *Physical violence in American families*. New Brunswick, NJ: Transaction.

Straus, M., & Gelles, R. (1986). Societal change and change in family violence from 1975-1985 as revealed by two national surveys. *Journal of Marriage and the Family, 48,* 465-479.

Sue, D. W., & Sue, D. (1990). *Counseling the culturally different: Theory and practice*. New York: John Wiley.

Sugarman, D., & Hotaling, G. (1989). Violent men in intimate relationships: An analysis of risk markers. *Journal of Applied Social Psychology, 19,* 1034-1048.

Sugg, N. K., & Inui, T. (1992). Primary care physician's response to domestic violence: Opening Pandora's box. *Journal of the American Medical Association, 267,* 3157-3178.

Sullivan, C., Basta, J. Cheribeth, T., & Davidson, W. (1992). After the crisis: A needs assessment of women leaving a domestic violence shelter. *Violence and Victims, 7,* 267-275.

Sullivan, C., & Rumptz, M. (1994). Adjustment and needs of African-American women who utilized a domestic violence shelter. *Violence and Victims, 9,* 275-286.

Tallen, B. (1990). Twelve step programs: A lesbian feminist critique. *NWSA Journal, 2,* 390-407.

Teplin, L., Abram, K., & McClelland, G. (1994). Does psychiatric disorder predict violent crime among released jail detainees? A six-year longitudinal study. *American Psychologist, 49,* 335-347.

Tierney, K. J. (1982). The battered women movement and the creation of the wife beating problem. *Social Problems, 29,* 207-220.

Tolman, R. (1989). The development of a measure of psychological maltreatment of women by their male partners. *Violence and Victims, 4,* 159-177.

Tolman, R., & Bennett, L. W. (1990). A review of quantitative research on men who batter. *Journal of Interpersonal Violence, 5,* 87-118.

Torres, S. (1991). A comparison of wife abuse between two cultures: Perception, attitudes, nature, and extent. *Issues in Mental Health Nursing, 12,* 113-131.

Turner, S. F., & Shapiro, C. H. (1986). Battered women: Mourning the death of a relationship. *Social Work, 30,* 372-376.

Urquiza, A., Wyatt, G., & Root, M. (1994). Violence against women of color. *Violence and Victims, 9,* 203-206.

Waitzkin, H. (1989). A critical theory of medical discourse: Ideology, social control, and the processing of social context in medical encounters. *Journal of Health and Social Behavior, 30,* 220-239.

Walker, L. E. A. (1979). *The battered woman.* New York: Harper & Row.

Walker, L. E. A. (1984). *The battered woman syndrome.* New York: Springer.

Walker, L. E. A. (1989). Psychology and violence against women. *American Psychologist, 44,* 695-702.

Walker, L. E. A. (1992). Battered woman syndrome and self-defense. *Notre Dame Journal of Law, Ethics, and Public Policy, 6,* 321-334.

Walker, L. E. A. (1993). The battered woman syndrome is a psychological consequence. In R. Gelles & D. Loseke (Eds.), *Current controversies on family violence.* Newbury Park, CA. Sage.

Walker, L. E. A. (1994). *Abused women and survivor therapy.* Washington, DC: American Psychological Association.

Walker, L. E. A., & Browne, A. (1985). Gender and victimization by intimates. *Journal of Personality, 53,* 179-195.

Warshaw, C. (1989). Limitations of the medical model in the care of battered women. *Gender & Society, 3,* 506-517.

Warshaw, C. (1993). Domestic violence: Challenges to medical practice. *Journal of Women's Health, 2,* 73-80.

Warshaw, C. (1995a). Violence and women's health: Old models, new challenges. In Center for Mental Health Services, *Dare to vision: Shaping the national agenda for women, abuse and mental health services.* Holyoke, MA: Human Resources Association.

Warshaw, C. (1995b). Establishing an appropriate response to domestic violence in your practice, institution and community. In D. Lee, N. Durborow, & P. Salber (Eds.), *Improving the health care response to domestic violence: A resource manual for health care providers.* San Francisco: Family Violence Prevention Fund.

Weick, A., Rapp, C., Sullivan, W., & Kisthardt, W. (1989). A strengths perspective for social work practice. *Social Work, 34,* 350-354.

Wilson, M., & Daly, M. (1993). Spousal homicide risk and estrangement. *Violence and Victims, 8,* 3-16.

Worell, J., & Remer, P. (1992). *Feminist perspectives in therapy: An empowerment model for women.* New York: John Wiley.

Zubrestsky, T., & Digirotama, K. (1996). The false connection between adult domestic violence and alcohol. In A. Roberts (Ed.), *Helping battered women: New perspectives and remedies.* New York: Oxford University Press.

Index

Abram, K., 144, 178
Abuse history:
    contributions, 72, 73
    questions, 76
    tools, 73
    verification, 75-77
Abusive behaviors, 74, 75, 140
Ackerman, R. J., 14, 169
Adams, D., 133, 151, 169
Addiction Severity Index, 67
Admitters, 136
Advocacy programs, 158
African-American women, 115, 119-121
Agency, 137
Alcoholics Anonymous (AA), 29
Allen, P., 125, 169
Anger management programs, 151
Anspach, R. R., 16, 17, 90, 169
Anwar, R., 13, 20, 30, 37, 68, 69, 175
Appelbaum, P. S., 9, 169
Arias, I., 70, 169
Asian women, 115, 126-128
Assessment, 65-94
    abuse history, 72-77
    assessment instruments, 69-72
    diagnosis. See Diagnosis
    reporting/documentation, 90-92

    safety planning, 77-79
    screening questions, 68, 69
Assessment instruments, 69-72
Astin, M. C., 86, 88, 169
Attributional shift, 73
Avoidance strategies, 145-148
Avoiding your partner, 82
Axis IV diagnosis, 86, 89

Bakerman, R., 122, 176
Barriers, 14-20
Basta, J., 77, 178
Battered woman syndrome (BWS), 88
Batterer programs, 149-152
Batterers, 132-156
    abusive behaviors, 74, 75, 140
    admitters, 136
    assessment issues, 132, 133
    avoidance strategies, 145-148
    clinical response, 145-154
    confronting denial, 136-140
    cost-benefit analysis, 148, 149
    counseling (batterer) programs, 149-152
    dangerousness, 142, 143
    denial/minimization, 134-136
    identifying, 134-140

informing battered woman, 152-154
profiles, 141, 142
questioning, 136-138
righteous crime, 144, 145
safety concerns, 133, 134
sources of evidence, 136-139
typologies, 142
Battle fatigue, 98
Beach, S., 70, 169
Beckett, J., 119, 121, 171
Bell, C., 121, 169
Bennett, L. W., 150, 178
Bibliography, 163-168
Binder, R. L., 45, 169
Bland, R., 8, 143, 170
Bograd, M., 11, 170
Bonilla-Santiago, G., 124, 170
Bowker, L., 12, 77, 88, 170
Brown, L. S., 85, 170
Browne, A., 12, 30, 72, 81, 85, 86, 95-98, 100, 101, 103, 105, 106, 114, 170, 179
BWS, 88

Campbell, D., 114, 119, 170
Campbell, J., 70, 114, 119, 170, 177
Campbell, J. C., 78, 81, 82, 88, 89, 170
Campbell, R., 83, 84, 170
Caplan, G., 28, 170
Caplan, P., 28, 170
Carmen, E., 19, 83, 89, 100, 101, 103, 176
Carver, C. S., 96, 170, 177
Casas, J. M., 117, 176
Cascardi, M., 83, 98, 171
Case consultation, 24
Case studies, 43-64
    Debra (commitment of battered woman), 45-48
    Judy (evaluation of woman with multiple problems), 55-62
    Pam (evaluation of recently battered woman), 48-55
    source/context of cases, 44, 45
Cazenave, N., 119, 171
Chamberlin, J., 102, 171
Chesler, P., 102, 171
Chester, B., 124-126, 171
Chu, J., 85, 171
Clinical reports, 90-92
Coley, S., 119, 121, 171

Collaboration, 23-39
Alcoholics Anonymous, 29
basic ingredients, 31
community mental health movement, 28, 29
cooperative efforts, 27
existing cooperation, 24-28
immediate steps, 30
implementation aids, 33, 34
individual initiatives, 31-33
institutional support, 34-36
program linkages, 36-38
referral/case consultation, 24-26
Community mental health centers (CMHCs), 29
Community mental health movement, 28, 29
Computerized record system of battering, 92
Confidentiality, 153
Conflict Tactic Scale, 72
Conrad, P., 8, 171
Consultations, 24
Coping strategies, 98
Cost-benefit analysis, 148, 149
Couples counseling/couples groups, 151
Cowger, C., 95, 96, 171
Crenshaw, K., 114, 120, 171
Crimes of passion, 144
Cross-cultural issues, 113-131
    African-American women, 115, 119-121
    Asian women, 115, 126-128
    clinical responses to racial/ethic diversity, 116
    current approaches, 117, 118
    immigrant women, 115, 128-131
    Latina women, 115, 122-124
    manuals, 117
    Native American women, 115, 124-126
Culver, D. M., 47, 177

Daly, M., 77, 179
Dangerousness assessments, 142, 143
Davis, L., 117, 134, 171, 176
Deegan, P., 102, 171
Deniers, 134-136
Denzin, N. K., 29, 171
Depressive disorders, 83, 84

Deterrents to reporting, 44, 45
Development linkages, 37, 38
Diagnosis:
  battered woman syndrome, 88
  common diagnoses, 83-86
  depressive disorders, 83, 84
  dissociative disorder, 84
  issues, 79-81
  meaning of symptoms, 81, 84
  personality disorders, 85
  process, 89
  PTSD, 85-88
Differences in perspective, 5-14
Digirotama, K., 145, 179
Dill, D., 85, 171
Dissociative disorder, 84
Diversity among battered women. *See*
  Cross-cultural issues
Dobash, R. E., 6, 7, 171
Dobash, R. P., 6, 7, 171
Douglas, M. A., 88, 171
Dunham, H. W., 29, 171
Dutton, D. G., 141, 171
Dutton, M. A., 12, 19, 65, 66, 72, 73, 75, 81,
  86, 89, 96, 100, 101, 171, 172
Duty to warn, 154

Edleson, J., 12, 70, 135, 141, 150, 152, 157,
  158, 172
Eisikovits, Z. C., 141, 150, 172
Emotional abuse, 75
Empowerment counseling, 96
Environmental supports, 33
Evaluation process, 16-18

Family counseling, 9, 10
Family Violence Prevention Fund, 34
Ferraro, K., 99, 172
Financial control, 74
Fisher, E. R., 73, 88, 89, 96, 98, 103, 104,
  122, 173
Fisher, S., 16, 18, 90, 172
Flaskerud, J., 118, 172
Flitcraft, A., 28, 85, 178
Follow-up questions, 69
Fossum, M., 14, 172
Foster, R., 32, 135, 137, 172, 173
Foy, D. W., 86, 174

Frank, P., 30, 172
Frankl, V., 104, 172
Funnel questioning, 138

Gamache, D., 158, 172
Geffner, R., 172
Gelles, R., 148, 172
Girder, L., 68, 172
Gleason, W. J., 81, 172
Goldstein, J., 95-97, 172
Gondolf, E. W., 7, 8, 11, 16, 17, 19, 28, 30,
  32, 37, 44, 66, 68, 73, 76, 78, 80, 81, 85,
  88, 90, 92, 96, 98, 103, 104, 118, 122,
  129, 132, 133, 135, 137, 138, 141, 142,
  144-146, 148, 150, 153, 172, 173
Goodman, L., 12, 84, 96, 101, 102, 113, 127,
  175
Gordon-Bradshaw, R. H., 120, 173
Gottman, J., 142, 173
Grieving process, 83, 100
Guillebeaux, F., 136, 173

Hagen, J., 134, 171
Hamberger, L. K., 142-144, 173
Hammer, M., 14, 173
Hansen, J., 134, 174
Hansen, M., 11, 173
Hart, B., 77-80, 82, 133, 141, 142, 151, 173,
  174
Hartman, C., 133, 136, 174
Harway, M., 134, 174
Hasting, J. E., 142-144, 173
Hawkins, D., 121, 174
Herman, J. L., 12, 19, 80, 81, 85, 88,
  100-102, 174
Ho, C. K., 127-129, 174
Hodson, C., 99, 175
Holamon, B., 119, 122, 176
Holtzworth-Munroe, A., 73, 142, 174
Horwitz, M., 75, 174
Hotaling, G., 142, 178
Housekamp, B. M., 86, 174
Hudson, W., 70, 93, 137, 174
Huisman, K., 127, 128, 174

Identifying men who batter. *See* Batterers
Immigrant women, 115, 128-131

Impact of Event Scale, 75
In-depth psychodynamic programs, 151
Index of Spouse Abuse (ISA), 70, 71, 73, 137
Individual initiatives, 31-33
Informing battered women, 152-154
Intimidation, 74
Inui, T., 18, 178
Isolation, 74
Items required for leaving, 83

Jackson, T., 134, 176
Jacobson, A., 37, 44, 68, 72, 174
Jacobson, N., 142, 173
Jang, D., 127, 129, 174
Janoff-Bulman, R., 80, 81, 174
Jasinski, J., 122, 123, 174
Johnson, J., 99, 172
Jones, A., 34, 174
Jones-Brown, C., 37, 174
Jouriles, E. N., 135, 174
Justifications, 135

Kadison, G., 30, 172
Kantor, G., 122, 123, 174
Kasl, C., 30, 174
Katz, J., 144, 175
Kaufman, G., 11, 175
Keane, T., 75, 175
Kemp, A., 81, 175
Kilpatrick, D. G., 68, 177
Kivel, P., 135, 175
Koehler, J., 44, 68, 174
Koss, M., 12, 84, 96, 101, 102, 113, 127, 175
Kuipers, J. C., 17, 175
Kurz, D., 16, 175

Latina women, 115, 122-124
Lawrence, K. J., 86, 169
Lethality checklist, 78, 79
Lidz, C., 17, 70, 175, 176
Lifton, R., 99, 175
Linkages, 36-38
Loseke, D., 119, 175
Luborsky, L., 67, 175

Lum, D., 117, 175

Machismo, 122
Mahoney, M., 85, 175
Malloy, P., 75, 175
Maltreatment of Women Scale, 72
Marin, B., 123, 175
Marin, G., 123, 175
Marinism, 122
Marolla, J., 136, 177
Marshall, L., 68, 70, 175
Masochistic, 98
McFarlane, J., 68, 175
McIntosh, S., 70, 93, 137, 174
McLeer, S. V., 13, 20, 30, 37, 68, 69, 175
McLellan, A. T., 67, 175
McNiel, D., 45, 169
Medical model, 8, 9
Medical sociology, 16
Mental illness, 101, 102
Mercy, J., 119, 176
Meth, R., 136, 175
Mills, T., 99, 175
Minimizations, 134, 135
Mishler, E., 16, 175
Mitchell, R., 99, 175
MMPI-2, 75
Monitoring and reviews, 35
Moore, S., 88, 176
Morash, M., 123, 177
Morrison, E., 70, 176
Mulvey, E., 17, 70, 175, 176
Murphy, C. M., 135, 176

National Resource Center on Domestic Violence, 34
National Resource Center on Domestic Violence survey, 5, 158-162
Native American women, 115, 124-126
Neff, J., 119, 122, 176
Neighbors, H., 118, 176
New model, 12-14
Nowotny, M. L., 96, 176

Obtaining information, 32
O'Carroll, P., 119, 176

O'Leary, K. D., 83, 98, 135, 171, 174
Options for woman, 152
Organizational barriers, 14-20
Orn, H., 8, 143, 170

Parker, B., 68, 175
Pasick, R., 136, 175
Paymar, M., 73, 74, 133, 135, 139, 176
Peck, M. S., 14, 176
Pence, E., 73, 74, 133, 135, 139, 151, 176
Perilla, J., 122, 176
Perrin, S., 89, 172
Personality disorders, 85
Perspectives, differences in, 5-14
Petretic-Jackson, P., 134, 176
Physical abuse, 75
Ponterotto, J., 117, 176
Positive self-talk, 147
Posttraumatic stress disorder (PTSD),
    85-88
Power and control wheel, 73
Powers, M., 125, 176
Proctor, E., 117, 176
Professional status, 18, 19
Program linkages, 36-38
Protection orders, 82
Protocol, 19, 20, 30
Protocol checklists, 34
Protocol monitoring and review, 35
Psychiatric survivors, 102
Ptacek, J., 145, 176
PTSD, 85-88

Race/ethnicity. See Cross-cultural issues
Raising awareness, 32
Rapp, C., 95, 179
Rappaport, J., 118, 176
Rawlings, E. I., 81, 175
Recommended bibliography, 163-168
Redefining symptoms, 81, 84, 98
References, 169-179
Referrals, 24
Reframing, 104
Relationship problems, 9, 10
Remer, P., 79, 96, 179
Reporting, 90-92
Retraining and evaluation, 35

Reynolds, D., 133, 136, 174
Richardson, B., 68, 174
Richie, B., 120, 176
Riecker, P., 44, 170
Rieker, P., 19, 89, 103, 176
Riggs, D. S., 135, 176
Righteous crime, 144, 145
Robin, R., 124-126, 171
Rose, K., 37, 177
Rumptz, M., 119, 120, 178
Russell, D., 146, 173
Russell, L., 69, 177
Russell, M. N., 135, 177

Safety planning:
    avoiding your partner, 82
    items required for leaving, 83
    overview, 77-79
    planning guide, 80
    protection orders, 82
Safety with protection orders, 82
Saleebey, D., 95, 97, 177
Santiago, A., 123, 177
Saunders, B. E., 68, 177
Saunders, D., 11, 37, 65, 66, 72, 78, 81, 86,
    142, 177
Schecter, S., 10, 19, 34, 79, 157, 174, 177
Scheff, T. J., 47, 177
Scheier, M. F., 96, 170, 177
Schmidt, J., 78, 177
Schneider, J., 8, 171
Screening and assessment protocols, 19,
    20
Screening questions, 68, 69
Scully, D., 136, 177
Segal, S. P., 45, 177
Self-talk, 146, 147
Self-transcendence, 104
Separation issues, 99, 100
Service linkages, 37, 38
Sexual abuse, 75
Shapiro, C. H., 83, 179
Shea, S. C., 9, 66, 177
Shepard, M., 70, 177
Sherman, L., 78, 177
Shestakov, D., 129, 173
Short-term anger management programs,
    151

Shupe, A., 12, 177
Simon, B., 96, 177
Simpatico, 122
Simpson, O.J., 114, 136
Social intervention, 11
Sonkin, D., 154, 177
Sorenson, S., 122, 123, 178
Soulfulness, 119
Stacey, W., 12, 177
Staff reminders, 33
Stanton, S., 14, 173
Stark, E., 28, 85, 178
Starzomski, A., 141, 171
Stefan, S., 102, 178
Stein, D., 129, 178
Steinman, M., 158, 178
Stille, R., 135, 178
Stoltenberg, J., 144, 178
Stordeur, R. A., 135, 178
Storm, C., 136, 173
Stosny, S., 133, 140, 178
Straus, M., 72, 119, 171
Strengths assessment, 95-109
    coping strategies, 98
    empowerment counseling, 96
    mental illness, 101, 102
    posttrauma effects, 100, 101
    relationship expectations, 99
    separation issues, 99, 100
    steps in, process, 109
    strengths inventory, 105-108
    survivor theory, 103-105
Stuart, R., 142, 174
Stuehling, J., 77, 78, 80, 82
Sue, D., 117, 127-129, 178
Sue, D. W., 117, 127-129, 178
Sugarman, D., 142, 178
Sugg, N. K., 18, 178
Sullivan, C., 77, 82, 84, 119, 120, 170, 178
Survey of state coalitions of battered
    women's programs, 5, 158-162
Survivor theory, 103

Syers, M., 70, 135, 172
Symptoms, redefining, 81, 84, 98

Tallen, B., 30, 178
Telles, C., 122, 123, 178
Teplin, L., 144, 178
Tierney, K. J., 10, 178
Tolman, R., 12, 72, 150, 152, 172, 178
Torres, S., 122, 178
Triple jeopardy, 120
Turner, S. F., 83, 179
Types/tactics of woman abuse, 74, 75

Urquiza, A., 114, 116, 179

V codes, 9
Victim-perpetrator intervention, 11
Visible supports for women, 34

Waiting-room brochures, 34
Waitzkin, H., 16, 17, 90, 179
Walker, L. E. A., 10-12, 77, 85, 88, 96, 98,
    101, 103, 179
Warshaw, C., 8, 13, 18-20, 30, 33, 68, 72, 73,
    76, 88, 90, 92, 179
Watson, M. A., 45, 177
Weick, A., 95, 179
When Love Goes Wrong: What to Do When
    You Can't Do Anything Right, 34
Wilner, N., 75, 174
Wilson, M., 77, 179
Woman battering perspective, 10, 11
Woman battering protocol, 19, 20, 30
Worrell, J., 79, 96, 179
Wyatt, G., 114, 116, 179

Zubrestsky, T., 145, 179

About the Authors

Edward W. Gondolf, EdD, MPH, is Professor of Sociology at Indiana University of Pennsylvania (IUP) and Associate Director of Research for the Mid-Atlantic Addiction Training Institute (MAATI). At MAATI, he conducts funded research on the relationship of alcohol abuse to domestic violence and the response of the civil court, domestic violence court, medical practitioners, and alcohol treatment clinicians to domestic violence. He recently served as Research Consultant to the National Resource Center for Domestic Violence funded by a 3-year grant from the U.S. Department of Health and Human Services, and continues to serve on the advisory board of the National Domestic Violence Hotline.

Dr. Gondolf has authored six books on wife abuse, including *Men Who Batter: An Integrated Approach to Stopping Wife Abuse* (1985), *Battered Women as Survivors: An Alternative to Treating Learned Helplessness* (1988), *Psychiatric Response to Family Violence: Identifying and Confronting Neglected Danger* (1990), as well as over 60 research articles on men who batter and community development. *Psychiatric Response*, based on a study funded by the National Institute of Mental Health (NIMH), analyzes data from 382 psychiatric patients to document the clinical neglect of reported family violence in favor of identifying mental disorders.

Angela Browne, PhD, is a social psychologist with expertise in the area of family violence. During the 1980s, she conducted research on cases in which battered women kill their abusers in self-defense and authored the book *When Battered Women Kill* (1987). Since 1988, she has acted as Consulting Psychologist to Bedford Hills Maximum Security Prison for women in New York State. She has authored numerous articles and book chapters, including both the American Medical Association's and the American Psychological Association's review and policy statements on violence against women, as well as the National Academy of Sciences' report on violence between intimates. She is a coauthor of *No Safe Haven: Male Violence Against Women at Home, at Work, and in the Community* (1994).

Susan Schechter is Clinical Professor at the University of Iowa School of Social Work and a research associate at the university's Injury Prevention Research Center. She is the author of several books and monographs about domestic violence, including *Women and Male Violence: The Visions and Struggles of the Battered Women's Movement, When Love Goes Wrong,* (coauthored with Ann Jones), and *Guidelines for Mental Health Practitioners in Domestic Violence Cases.* She has directed and founded several clinical and advocacy programs, including AWAKE, Advocacy for Women and Kids in Emergencies at Children's Hospital, Boston, which is the first program in a pediatric hospital for battered women with abused children. She is currently a consultant to the National Resource Center on Domestic Violence and to the Family Violence Prevention Fund's Family Preservation—Domestic Violence Curriculum project and its Domestic Violence-Child Protection project.